SO-BBD-469

# Modern
# Political
# Philosophy

# EXPLORATIONS IN PHILOSOPHY

## James H. Fetzer, Series Editor

**Aesthetics**
*James W. Manns*

**Social Philosophy**
*Gerald F. Gaus*

**Modern Political Philosophy**
*Richard Hudelson*

EXPLORATIONS
in philosophy

# Modern
# Political
# Philosophy

## Richard Hudelson

*M.E. Sharpe*
Armonk, New York
London, England

**Library of Congress Cataloging-in-Publication Data**

Hudelson, Richard.
Modern political philosphy / Richard Hudelson.
p.   cm.—(Explorations in philosophy)
Includes bibliographical references and index.
ISBN 0-7656-0021-8 (cloth : alk. paper)
1. Political science—Philosophy—History.  I. Title.  II. Series
JA83.H84    1999
320.5—dc21        98-56178
CIP

Printed in the United States of America

The paper used in this publication meets the minimum requirements of
American National Standard for Information Sciences—
Permanence of Paper for Printed Library Materials,
ANSI Z 39.48-1984.

BM (c)    10    9    8    7    6    5    4    3    2

*To Rachel and Alicia*

# Contents

# Series Foreword

The series *Explorations in Philosophy* is intended to provide un-
dergraduates and other readers with quality introductions not only to
the principal areas of philosophy, including traditional topics of inves-
tigation—epistemology, ethics, and social and political philosophy—
but also to contemporary subjects of importance—such as critical
theory, feminist studies, and the ethics of reproduction. In each case,
the editors have chosen authors who could not only explain the central
problems encountered within their respective domains but who could
also propose promising solutions to those problems, including novel
approaches and original analyses.

The present volume, *Modern Political Philosophy*, explores the
nature, principles, and rationale that underlie the exercise of government. The author, Richard Hudelson, begins with the dawn of a new
age represented by the Declaration of Independence and its affirmation
of human rights and ends with the contemporary challenge posed by
globalization, where transnational corporations owe allegiance to no
sovereign nation. Anyone who wants to understand the nuances of
political debate today ought to read this remarkable study. Of all the
books I have read, this one may be the most successful in achieving the
goals its author set himself. It is a marvelous introduction to political
philosophy.

James H. Fetzer

# Preface

Human beings are social animals. Like ants, bees, wolves, and other social animals, we depend upon others of our kind for our survival in this world. Like these other social animals, we live in groups, and our group life is organized into a system of social order. Different individuals play different roles, bearing the particular responsibilities attached to these roles. Among us, as among all of the social animals, interactions between individuals are governed by a system of more or less complicated rules. But unlike the other social animals, which replicate the ways of life of their ancestors, human beings are constantly changing their way of life. Other animals have relatively firm dispositions to obey the social rules of their kind genetically programmed into them. The form of their social life changes slowly, as a matter of natural history. For them, the form of their social life is a biological given. We, on the contrary, are historical creatures. We create the forms of our social existence in historical time. For us, the form of our social existence is a matter of deliberation and choice. It is the task of political philosophy to think about what form of social existence is best.

This book aims at providing the reader with an introduction to political philosophy. Unlike many other introductions to political philosophy, this book takes a historical approach to the subject. We will begin with the natural-rights theory of the American Revolution. Here the fundamental task of political philosophy is revealed with stark clarity, for political revolution involves both the rapid transformation of the fundamental rules of social existence and deliberation about what those fundamental rules should be. The philosophy of natural rights will thus serve as a model for what political philosophy is. But, like all things human, the philosophy of natural rights is itself subject to historical transformation. The theory of natural rights was subjected to criticism, and that criticism gave rise to utilitarianism, an entirely different approach to thinking about the question of what form of social existence is best. In the chapters of this book we will more or less follow the course of political philosophy from the time of the American Revolution up to the present.

There are several reasons for taking this approach. First, for the reader not familiar with political philosophy, this approach provides an accessible point of entry. The ideas of the American Declaration of Independence are already familiar to anyone reading this book. By following the elaboration of those ideas, the criticism of those ideas, and the rise of utilitarianism, the reader enters into the subject matter of political philosophy in a relatively painless way.

Second, I believe that political philosophy should address the real issues of the age. Philosophers must attempt more systematic and rigorous thinking than either politicians or journalists have time for. But philosophers should make some effort to address real problems, and this cannot be done well without some sense of the historical development that produced the present. The form of social life that we inherit from the past, with its laws and institutions, was created by our ancestors as a way of responding to the problems of their age. To now think seriously about what our laws and institutions should be, we need to understand the rationality of the past.

The reconstruction of the history of modern political philosophy in the chapters that follow is meant to provide the reader with some sense of this rationality of the past. However, the reader should keep in mind that the aim of this book is not to provide a history of modern political philosophy. That is, in a sense, the proper task of the historian. The task of political philosophy is to think about what the fundamental principles governing our society should be. This is a philosophical concern, not a historical one. But it is a question that can be seriously considered only from within a historical context, by people living at a specific location in history and facing a historically specific array of social problems.

Political philosophy considers what rules should govern our lives and what sorts of institutions we should create to enforce those rules. Answers to these questions require careful consideration of the principles of ethics, but also require considerations of human nature, of the social sciences, and of history. This book puts special emphasis on consideration of what should be the proper role of free markets in the fabric of the institutions that govern our lives. It does so because at this point in human history powerful forces are promoting free markets as foundations for the global institutions of an emerging new world order. Whether the treatment of this issue offered here is or is not adequate must, of course, be left to the reader to decide.

# Acknowledgments

I thank series editor James Fetzer for his support of this book and for his encouragement, criticism, and advice over the past decade. I also thank my colleagues Dale Miller, Russell Stewart, Steve Chilton, Khalil Dokhanchi, and Maria Cuzzo for their helpful comments on earlier versions of this work. I would also like to thank Susan Warga, whose editorial suggestions have made this a better book than it otherwise would have been.

# Modern
# Political
# Philosophy

# — Chapter 1 —

# Natural Rights

At ten o'clock on the night of April 18, 1775, seven hundred British soldiers under the command of Lieutenant Colonel Francis Smith began moving out of Boston. General Thomas Gage, commander in chief of British forces in North America, had commanded Colonel Smith to march "with the utmost expedition and secrecy to Concord, where you will seize and destroy all the artillery and ammunition you can find."[1] Marching at night, the soldiers could hear signal shots and the ringing of church bells as they made their way along the road toward Concord, the local residents having been warned of the coming of the British force by two dispatch riders, William Dawes and Paul Revere. Realizing that the element of surprise had been lost, Colonel Smith ordered Major John Pitcairn to go ahead with six companies of lightly armed fast infantry to try to prevent the aroused colonials from removing the military supplies from Concord.

At dawn on the morning of the nineteenth, Pitcairn's British forces encountered a group of some seventy or eighty minutemen, local colonial militia, under the command of Captain John Parker. The men were spread in a line across the village green in Lexington, a town lying along the road between Boston and Concord. The Americans, greatly outnumbered by the British, did not attempt to block the road and had begun an orderly withdrawal when, from one side or the other, a shot was fired. At the sound of the musket, British soldiers opened fire on the Americans. Before Pitcairn's shout to cease fire was obeyed, eight Americans had been killed and ten others had been wounded. There were no casualties on the British side.

The British force resumed its march to Concord. There the British entered the town without resistance and destroyed the few military supplies that had not been removed. After a brief exchange of fire between British and American forces at North Bridge, on the edge of Concord, with light casualties on both sides, Colonel Smith, considering his mission accomplished, ordered British troops to begin the march back to Boston. By now, however, enraged colonials from nearby towns and farms had taken up positions behind the trees and stone walls that lined the road. From these protected positions they fired at the red-coated British troops marching along the road. By dusk, when the British troops reached the safety of Charleston, more than 70 soldiers had been killed and 175 had been wounded.

What could possibly lead peaceful farmers and tradesmen to inflict deadly fire on a line of marching soldiers? To be sure, the killing of Americans at Lexington and Concord must have provoked great anger. But why did the Americans resist in the first place? Why were arms stored at Concord? Why did the local militia take up arms and line up across the green at Lexington?

The Lexington militia did not act in haste. Warned that the British were coming, they met in a tavern near the village green for several hours before the British arrived, where they discussed what to do.[2] Clearly the minutemen of Lexington believed that resistance to the British was right and that the issues involved were sufficiently important to kill or be killed for their sake.

In fact, the town of Lexington had been discussing these matters for some time. In 1765, when the British government passed the Stamp Act to raise revenues in the colonies, the town of Lexington voted to instruct its representative in the General Court of the colony to protest the act. The actual instruction sent by the town, setting out reasons why the act was unjust, was written by Jonas Clarke, a clergyman and prominent leader in Lexington. It was at Clarke's home where the colonial leaders Samuel Adams and John Hancock were staying on the night of the British expeditionary force's move against Lexington and Concord.

In the instruction that he had written for the people of Lexington, Clarke advanced a number of different reasons for thinking the Stamp Act was unjust. He claimed that it violated the ancient right of British subjects to be taxed only with their own consent. He also maintained that the act violated the agreement between British kings and their subjects enshrined in the Magna Carta. Finally, Clarke also held that the Stamp Act violated the rights and liberties of men who were "beings naturally free."[3] Clarke's appeal to the ancient rights of British subjects and his appeal to the Magna Carta justified resistance to the Stamp Act on historical and legal grounds. These reasons appealed to rights belonging to British subjects in virtue of their being British. Neither the ancient rights of British subjects nor the Magna Carta had anything to say about the rights of human beings who were not British subjects. By contrast, Clarke's third argument left behind the particular claims to rights that belonged to the American colonists in virtue of their being British subjects. It claimed rights as belonging to the Americans in virtue of their status as "beings naturally free." Here the justification of the claim to rights lies not in legal precedents established in the past but in the very nature of men as beings of a certain kind. Such rights are natural rights. They belong to men as men. (Clarke and his contemporaries did not even consider the rights of women.) They apply to Americans, to all other British subjects, to Frenchmen, to Chinese— to all men. Agreements such as the Magna Carta can create special rights, but natural rights are not created by any human agreement. They belong to men as beings having a certain nature.

In the years leading up to the American Revolution, the American colonists often appealed to the ancient rights of Englishmen embedded in the unwritten constitution that had supposedly governed English life from time immemorial. They appealed to the Magna Carta. They appealed to the specific rights guaranteed to the colonists in the charters granted by British kings in founding the American colonies. They also appealed to natural rights possessed by Americans simply in virtue of their nature as men. For example, a resolution adopted by the town of Lexington maintained that the keeping of a standing British army in the colonies to enforce the acts of Parliament was an infringement of the "natural, constitutional and chartered rights" of the colonists.[4] These different arguments were mutually supporting, but the natural-rights argument was fundamentally different in scope and kind. Appealing to neither history nor legal precedent, it raised directly philosophical reasons for resisting the authority of the British government, reasons that implied rights that were universal in scope, applying to all men everywhere. It was this directly philosophical claim to universal natural rights that made the shot on Lexington green, in the words of Ralph Waldo Emerson, "the shot heard 'round the world."

Not only for Americans, but also for people in all corners of the world, the Declaration of Independence, adopted by the Second Continental Congress in 1776, provides an inspiring and powerful formulation of the philosophy of natural rights:

> We hold these truths to be self-evident, that all men are created equal, that they are endowed by their Creator with certain unalienable Rights, that among these are Life, Liberty and the pursuit of Happiness. That to secure these rights, Governments are instituted among Men, deriving their just powers from the consent of the governed, that whenever any Form of Government becomes destructive of these ends, it is the Right of the People to alter or to abolish it, and to institute new Government.

In these words the American colonists appealed directly to rights endowed upon all men by their creator, to rights held by all men in virtue of their God-given nature as men. The American colonists did not invent this idea. The theory of natural rights has a long history running back to the works of the ancient Greek and Roman philosophers. Particularly influential on the thinking of the American colonists was the English philosopher John Locke, whose *Second Treatise* on government used a theory of natural rights to defend the English revolution of 1688. Indeed, the phrases of the Declaration so closely parallel passages from Locke that a fellow Virginian accused Thomas Jefferson, the principle author of the Declaration, of copying directly from Locke's *Second Treatise*.[5] In the discussion that follows we will sometimes turn to Locke and other philosophers in an attempt to make sense of some of the basic concepts of the philosophy of natural rights found in the Declaration.[6]

## Rights

The Declaration of Independence claims that men have certain rights. This idea of rights is clearly one of the basic ideas of the philosophy of natural rights. We Americans often argue about what rights there are. Is there, for example, a right to die? We also argue about who has certain rights. Does the fetus in the womb have a right to life? However, despite these differences, we tend to take the idea of rights for granted. We rarely stop to ask just what a right is or what it is for a person to have a right. Now, in fact, contemporary philosophy recognizes several different kinds of rights. We will consider some of these different kinds of rights in later chapters of this book. Here, though, we will focus on a particular conception of rights that is central to the philosophy of the Declaration and to the historical core of the philosophy of natural rights.

According to this conception, a right is a moral claim belonging to an individual that prohibits all other persons from acting in certain ways toward that individual. For example, your right to life prohibits all other persons from killing you. Similarly, your right to liberty prohibits all other persons from enslaving you, kidnapping you, or holding you prisoner against your will. Such rights are often said to be moral fences: They surround people and protect them from outside interference. They are said to be "negative rights" in that they stipulate things that other people may *not* do in their interactions with some individual. Your right to life says that I may not kill you. My right to liberty says that you may not enslave me.

Rights protect people from outside interference. But, of course, the protection afforded by rights is not always effective. People have been murdered. People have been enslaved. The natural-rights theory does not deny these unfortunate facts of life. What it does say is that murder and slavery are serious moral infractions. This is what is meant by saying that rights are moral claims or moral fences. They stipulate things that other people *should* not do to you. They specify limits on how we may rightly or justly interact with one another. They also provide the basis for complaints of unjust treatment, as when the American colonists in the Declaration of Independence pointed to a series of actions by the king of England as transgressions of their rights, transgressions that justified resistance to English rule.

## Natural Rights

The rights to life and liberty claimed by the Declaration prohibit people from killing or enslaving one another. In this respect these rights are like rights created by human beings. Human laws often prohibit certain kinds of actions. Murder and kidnapping are illegal. Human law forbids them, though of course this does not prevent their happening from time to time. Like the rights proclaimed in the Declaration, legal rights say how we should behave, which is not always how we do behave. Legal rights, like the rights of the Declaration, are prescriptive, not descriptive. Both prescribe certain behaviors. But since we humans sometimes fail to live up to these prescriptions, neither accurately describes how we invariably will behave. In these ways the rights claimed by the philosophy of natural rights are like legal rights. Nonetheless, there are some important differences. These differences are central to the idea of certain rights as *natural* rights.

The fundamental difference between natural rights and legal rights is that legal rights are created by human beings and natural rights are not. Human law may give me certain rights. For example, human law gives me the right to drive a car provided I meet certain requirements. Supposing I have met those requirements, no one may interfere with me in the lawful driving of my car. However, the legislature might decide to restrict nighttime driving for people with poor night vision, or it might, because of life-threatening problems of pollution, decide to ban automobile driving for all but emergency purposes. My right to drive a car is created by human law and may be modified or abolished by the action of a legislature composed of human beings. My natural rights are not like this.

Consider, for example, my natural right to life, a right I have independent of any human action. The Declaration says that I am endowed with this right by my creator. It belongs to me simply in virtue of my being a human being who, like all human beings, is created equally with a certain nature. It belongs to me by nature, not by human artifice. My natural right to life does not depend upon any human act of creation and cannot be taken away by any human action. Legal rights are created by human action and can be taken away by human action. An evil legislative body might pass a law denying me a legal right to life. The legislature might, correctly following the rules of parliamentary procedure, amend the human law to permit the killing of human beings of a certain kind. Something like this happened in Germany in the 1930s, when the law was changed to deny civil rights to Jews. In America, of course, any such action would violate the written constitution that governs what our legislators may do. Such an action would be illegal because it violated my constitutional rights. But suppose a constitutional amendment is passed excluding human beings with my ethnic background from the protections of the Constitution. It would then be within the power of a human legislature to take away my right to life and the right to life of all people like me. However, according to natural-rights theory, while the legislature may have stripped me of my legal right to life, it would be wrong for it to do so.

The idea of a natural right to life can be easily grasped by reflecting on the debate over abortion that has divided Americans for the last quarter century. On one side, the state legislatures and the courts have said that abortion, subject to some restrictions, is legal. The law does not recognize a fetal right to life. On the other side, opponents of abortion argue that abortion is a great moral evil because it involves the violation of a natural right to life that belongs to every human fetus. Now, not all natural-rights theorists would agree that human fetuses do have a natural right to life. Here there is important disagreement about who is included among the class of beings that have a right to life. However, thinking about the abortion controversy can help us see what is involved in claiming such a right. The fetal right to life is supposed to be a natural right. Such rights do not depend upon human creation, and while they may be violated, they cannot be destroyed by any human action.

## Natural Law

We have already seen that natural rights are in some ways like legal rights. Both prohibit other people from interfering with us in certain ways. Both involve a complex network of responsibilities corresponding to the rights they claim. My natural right to life imposes a duty on you and all others to refrain from killing me. My right to drive a car imposes a duty on you and all others to refrain from interfering with my lawful exercise of that right. Legal rights exist as part of a system of laws. My legal right to drive a car and the corresponding duties of other persons are precisely spelled out by the laws governing the use of motor vehicles. In a similar way, natural-rights theorists conceive of natural rights as existing within a system of natural laws. The Declaration of Independence itself mentions "the laws of nature and nature's god" as the basis for those rights to life, liberty, and the pursuit of happiness it goes on to claim.

These laws of nature are moral laws. They are not like the laws of nature discovered by physics and chemistry, which tell us how things invariably do act but say nothing about how things *should* act. Unlike the laws of chemistry and physics, but like human-created legal laws, moral laws of nature are prescriptive rather than descriptive. They tell us how we ought to behave, not how we invariably do behave.

Like many natural-rights theorists, the authors of the Declaration of Independence saw the laws of nature as God's laws. The Declaration conceives of natural rights as part of a larger system of natural law, a body of moral law coming from God rather than from any human legislators. It is important, however, to distinguish this "natural law" from what philosophers and theologians have traditionally called "revealed law." The biblical text known as the Ten Commandments serves as an excellent example of revealed law. According to the biblical story, these commandments were given directly to Moses by God in an encounter on the top of Mount Sinai. In this story God reveals the commandments of the moral law to Moses and through him to all of God's chosen people. Preserved in the holy scriptures of the Jews, Christians, and Moslems, these commandments are then revealed to all who read them. The appearance of God before Moses on Mount Sinai is an example of a special revelation, an instance of God's speaking to a particular individual or group of individuals at a particular point in time. The revelation of God's message in the scriptures, available to all who can read them or hear them read, is an example of general revelation. Revealed law is based upon the general or special revelations of God's commandments that have appeared in the course of human history. In revealed law God's moral law appears to humans in the form of commandments given by a divine lawgiver.

While philosophers and theologians have generally agreed that the content of revealed law and the content of natural law are the same, the idea of natural law includes within it the idea that the moral law can be known by the use of human reason unassisted by either special or general revelation. For this reason natural-law philosophers have often spoken of natural law as the law of reason. Natural law is a system of moral laws that human beings can come to know by observing the nature of things and thereby discovering the right use of those things.

An example may help make this clear. It is of the nature of something that is a knife to have a sharp edge. Without a sharp edge suitable for cutting, a thing would not be a knife. Now, it is possible to use a knife in many different ways. It could be used to pry nails or as a doorstop, for example, but such uses would tend to damage the blade of the knife. For this reason they might be said to be contrary to the nature of the knife. Such uses are not the uses for which the nature of the knife is suited. On the other hand, to use the knife for cutting is to use it in accordance with its nature. The general idea of natural-law theory is that the right use of a thing is the use that is in accordance with its nature and that any use of a thing that is contrary to the nature of the thing is a wrong use of the thing.

Now, in this example there is surely no great moral wrong in using a knife to pry nails. But the example should help us see how important moral laws might be discoverable by examining the natures of things. Consider, for example, the nature of human beings. We are animals, and in this respect our nature shares some features with other animals. But human beings also have a capacity for thinking about what they are doing. Unless forced to change by changes in their environments, other animals replicate the ways of life of their ancestors. Humans, on the other hand, are constantly changing their ways of life. They think about their way of life and try to find better ways to satisfy their needs and better ways to express their thoughts and feelings. It is this capacity to think about what they are doing, to reflect upon their way of life, and to guide their lives by their thoughts that many philosophers have considered to be one of the distinctive features of human nature. Human beings are animals, but they are rational animals. Every normal human being has this capacity for thinking about his or her life and guiding that life by this thinking. This is a capacity that appears to be unique to human beings.

If this is so, we can begin to see how certain moral principles might be based on this human nature. How should we live our lives? What is the right use of a human life? Natural-law theory holds that we can begin to answer this question by studying our nature as human beings. Suppose we do that and, like the ancient Greeks, arrive at the conclusion that the nature of a human being is to be a rational animal. Then, according to the general principle that the right use of a thing is in accordance with its nature, it follows that the right use of our life requires us to think about our life and what we are doing. While it might be possible for a human being to live his or her life without ever stopping to think about it, such a life would fail to correspond to human nature. Even if it produced a life of success and great happiness, such a life would be, in some sense, subhuman. It would not be a life in accordance with our human nature. For this reason the philosopher Plato said in his *Apology* that "the unexamined life is not worth living for man."

Consider also the implications of this way of thinking about human nature for the institution of slavery. Suppose again that it is true that every normal human being has a capacity for thinking about his or her life and guiding that life by his or her own thinking. When we enslave human beings, we make them the subject of our will. We tell them what to do. In doing this we treat them as mere animals, lacking the power of rational self-direction. But, in doing this, we treat human beings contrary to their nature as human beings. In this way the natural-law thinker can argue that slavery is contrary to the law of nature. In this way also we can see how the natural right to liberty can be understood as a requirement of the natural law. Every normal human being has a capacity for rational self-direction. Consequently it is contrary to natural law to deprive a human being of the opportunity to exercise that capacity. We have a duty to refrain from such violations of the natural liberty of a person, and this, of course, is just what is meant in saying that a person has a natural right to liberty.

**Natural Equality**

We are now in a position to understand one of the most puzzling phrases in the Declaration of Independence. The Declaration says that "all men are created equal." But this seems to be patently untrue. Some men are wise; others are not. Some men are strong; others are weak. Isn't it obvious that human beings are very different from one another in these and other respects? How can the Declaration say not just that all men are equal but that this equality is self-evident? One common response here is to say that all the Declaration means in saying that all men are created equal is that all men have equal rights. But this response makes obscure the Declaration's two separate claims: one that all men are created equal and another that all men have certain rights. Further, this response misses entirely the connection between these two claims, the connection between human nature and natural rights discussed above. This connection is central to the whole idea of natural law.

In considering the idea of natural law, we saw how the right use of a thing is supposed to be connected to the nature of the thing. According to this view, slavery is wrong because it involves treating a human being with a capacity for rational self-direction in the way that one would treat an animal that lacked this capacity. In this view, the right to liberty that slavery violates is a natural right inherent in the very nature of a human being as a rational animal. It is this conception that lies behind the words of the Declaration. All men are created equal in the sense that all men have the capacity for rational self-direction, and it is because all men have this capacity that all have the equal right to liberty. This connection between an equality of rights and a prior equality of nature upon which the equality of rights depends is clearly formulated by Locke in the *Second Treatise,* where he says that there is "nothing more evident than that Creatures of the same species and rank promiscuously born to all the same advantages of Nature, and the use of the same faculties, should also be equal one amongst another without Subordination or Subjection."[7] The same idea, that an equality of rights is based upon a prior equality of nature, is also clearly present in the rough draft of the Declaration of Independence written by Thomas Jefferson. There the key philosophical section reads as follows:

> We hold these truths to be self-evident; that all men are created equal & independent, that from that equal creation they derive rights inherent & inalienable, among which are the preservation of life, & liberty & the pursuit of happiness.[8]

The equality of men is an equality of kind. All men are equal in the sense that they are all members of one kind and as such share in the nature of that kind. Because a capacity for rational self-direction is part of our nature as human beings, natural law requires that we be treated in accordance with that nature. Our natural right to liberty is thus a consequence of a distinct equality of nature, an equality of kind.

## Inalienable Rights

Inalienable rights are often thought to be rights that cannot be taken from us. A more accurate view would be that inalienable rights are rights that we may not relinquish. In the legal terminology of the eighteenth century, to alienate a thing was to transfer one's rights over it to some other person. To have property rights in a thing was to have the exclusive rights to use, sell, bequeath, or destroy the thing. Some or all of these rights could be transferred to another person. Thus the rights of ownership over a horse might be alienated by selling the horse or giving it away. While in those days laws of entailment restricted the transfer of some landed property, these restrictions were created by human law and applied only with respect to some property. For the most part, property other than land could be alienated by its owner at will. Alienation of one's rights over a horse involves the alienation of legal rights of ownership, rights that are created by human laws. While many interesting moral problems may arise in considering the rightness or wrongness of specific transfers of property rights, there seems to be no fundamental difficulty in the idea of the alienability of such rights. But when we come to our natural rights, there does seem to be a fundamental difficulty.

Consider my natural right to liberty. May I alienate this right? May I give up this right and transfer it to some other person? May I sell myself into slavery? If I do so, am I not treating myself contrary to my nature? The law of nature is based on the nature of things. Partaking of the nature of human kind, I share the capacity of rational self-direction. According to the natural law, I have a moral obligation to live in conformity to this nature. I have a moral obligation to use my capacity for rational self-direction. If I sell myself into slavery, I fail to live up to the requirements of the law of nature. For this reason, I may not alienate my right to liberty. Unlike the property rights I hold in a horse, my right to liberty is an inalienable right. By similar reasoning, it would seem that all my natural rights are inalienable. Since I have those rights in virtue of my God-given nature, I, like everyone else, am obliged by the law of nature to respect those rights in myself. Thus the Declaration of Independence holds that when a people confronts a despotic attempt to rule over them, "it is their right, it is their duty, to throw off such Government."

## Self-Evident Rights

The Declaration of Independence holds that it is "self-evident" that all men are created equal and that they are endowed by their creator with certain inalienable rights. With this idea of "self-evident" truths we encounter one of the more esoteric aspects of the philosophy of natural rights embedded in the Declaration. We can begin to see what is involved in the idea of self-evidence by considering systems such as the geometry developed by the ancient Greek astronomer Euclid. In Euclid's system a certain theorem of geometry is proven to be true by showing that it follows necessarily from theorems that have already been proven to be true. If we ask how we know that these earlier theorems are true, the answer is that they follow from other theorems that already have been proven to be true. In this way the truth of each theorem can be shown to follow from what has already been proven to be true. But it is obvious that such reliance upon prior results cannot be continued indefinitely. The whole system must begin somewhere. In the geometry of Euclid it begins with certain axioms. These axioms state the fundamental principles from which the truth of all other theorems are ultimately derived. But how can we know that these axioms are true? If we appeal to some other principles as evidence for the truth of our axioms, we merely postpone the difficulty, since now the question arises as to how we know that these other principles are true.

One way of solving this difficulty, of bringing the demand for justification to an end, is to say that these axioms are self-evident. What is meant by this is that anyone who truly understands what an axiom is saying will see that it simply must be true. It requires no evidence outside itself to support it. Its truth is manifest in itself. Consider, for example, the principle that equals added to equals give equals. The truth of this principle is transparent to anyone who understands what it says. It needs no proof, no external evidence. It is self-evident. Its truth is so clear and certain that no additional evidence could make it more evident to us than it already is.

Like many other philosophers, John Locke believed that in principle it was possible to construct a system of ethics that, like the mathematics of Euclid, would begin with self-evident axioms and derive from them a complete account of the principles of morality. He described the knowledge of such self-evident truths as being "like bright sunshine" that "forces itself immediately to be perceived, as soon as ever the mind turns its view that way; and leaves no room for hesitation, doubt, or examination, but the mind is presently filled with the clear light of it."[9] Despite his repeated assurances that such a project was in principle possible, that the laws of nature could be known by the methods of geometry, Locke himself never provided us with anything like a deductive system of ethics. Nonetheless, we have already considered some comments he made in the *Second Treatise* that throw some light on the claim to self-evident truth found in the Declaration of Independence.

Recall that in the *Second Treatise* Locke claimed that there was "nothing more evident" than that creatures of the same species "should also be equal one amongst another without subordination of subjection." In the section that immediately follows this remark, Locke goes on to cite the similar view of Richard Hooker, another philosopher of the natural law, that it is "evident in it self" that the equality of men by nature is the foundation of our moral obligations to one another.[10] In effect Locke and, in Locke's view, Hooker are saying that it is self-evident that men are equal by nature and self-evident that because men are equal by nature they have equal rights. These two claims about self-evident principles are the same two claims made by Jefferson in the rough draft of the Declaration, where he held that it was self-evident that "all men are created equal & independent" and self-evident that "from that equal creation they derive rights." The revised final version of the Declaration to some extent obscures the connection between these claims, saying only that two truths are self-evident: that all men are created equal and that all are endowed by their creator with certain inalienable rights. Nonetheless, it seems fairly clear that an understanding of the claims to self-evidence made by the Declaration will require an understanding of how the claim to natural equality could be thought to be self-evident and an understanding of how it could be thought to be self-evident that such an equality implied an equality of rights.

The first claim, that it is self-evident that all men are created equal, can be understood in a relatively straightforward way. If we think that men are by nature rational animals, then only those things that are rational animals are men. To say that all men are created equal is just to say that everything that is a man has the nature of being a rational animal. But this is like saying that all bachelors are unmarried males. Just as no thing could be a bachelor without being an unmarried male, so no thing could be a man without being a rational animal. "All men are created equal" is self-evident in the way that "All bachelors are unmarried" is self-evident. Once we understand what is being said, we see that it must be true.

The view that it is also self-evident that because all men are created equal they therefore have equal rights can be understood as a special instance of the fundamental idea of natural law. According to natural-law theory, given an understanding of the nature of a thing, we can derive from that how that thing should be used. But if this is true, since all men have the same nature, it would follow that all men should be treated in the same way—that all men have equal natural rights.

## Universal Rights

The natural rights claimed by the American revolutionaries were claimed on behalf of all men. They belonged to Americans, Englishmen, Frenchmen, and Chinese. In this sense, the rights claimed were universal rights, as opposed to the particular rights of Englishmen, rooted in the particular traditions of the English people. But in another sense, the rights claimed were not truly universal. They did not include women or males of African descent who labored as slaves in the land of freedom. We will consider the implications of these exclusions later in this book. Still, in a world largely ruled by tyrannical minorities, the Declaration's claim that every man had both a right and a duty to resist tyranny, despite its false universality, had revolutionary implications. From the great upheaval of the French Revolution, which soon followed the American example, to the massive demonstrations by students in Tiananmen Square in Beijing two hundred years later, the philosophical doctrine of natural rights has been a powerful force in history. Indeed, even those excluded by the American revolutionaries, such as women and Africans, would eventually appeal to the philosophy of natural rights to support their own claims to freedom and equality. In the chapters that follow we will examine some criticisms of the theory of natural rights. We will also look at some alternative ways of thinking about the fundamental issues of political life, and we will explore some of the ways that the theory of natural rights has been revised or expanded in response to these criticisms and alternative ways of thinking.

# — Chapter 2 —

# Utilitarianism

The theory of natural rights espoused by the Declaration of Independence defends the revolutionary political action of the American colonists. The Declaration claims that resistance to British rule was justified, and even required, by fundamental principles of the natural laws of morality. The Declaration of Independence appeared in July of 1776. That same year saw the publication of *An Inquiry into the Nature and Causes of the Wealth of Nations,* written by the Scottish philosopher Adam Smith. The relationship between the ideas of the Declaration and the ideas formulated by Smith in *The Wealth of Nations* is complex. As professor of moral philosophy at the University of Glasgow, Smith had begun to develop a system of ethics that was in its foundations radically different from the system of natural law espoused by the Declaration. However, while Smith's alternative system of ethics is clearly lurking in the background of *The Wealth of Nations,* that work is not itself devoted to the problems of moral philosophy. Its central concern is the science of economics. In this chapter we will examine both Adam Smith's science of economics and the ethical theory suggested by him.

**Smith's Economics**

How can a nation maximize the wealth it produces? This is the central question addressed by Adam Smith in *The Wealth of Nations.* Imagine a society in which each household produces everything it consumes. Each family grows its own food, makes its own clothing and shelter, and by its own labor supplies all its other needs. Such a society is scarcely imaginable. Under difficult conditions, where the climate was harsh or the soil poor, the household might devote all its waking hours to labor and still not survive. Under favorable conditions the household might survive, but its productive capacities would be limited to the boundaries of its own knowledge, skill, and resources. Now imagine a society in which households trade with one another. One specializes in growing food while another makes clothing and a third builds houses. With such a division of labor each household becomes more adept at the task assigned to it, and as a result the total amount of wealth produced by the society engaged in trade exceeds the total amount of wealth produced by the society in which each household provides for itself. With trade and increased production, the share available to each person is greater than it otherwise would be, and each party benefits.

Trade and the division of labor thus constitute important sources of wealth. Smith also sees a system of free markets as conducive to the wealth of a nation. A system of free markets is a system in which each individual is free to enter into contracts with any other individual to buy or sell goods or labor power. Within such a market system buyers will look for sellers offering goods at the lowest price, and sellers will look for buyers willing to pay the most for the goods they have to sell. With buyers and sellers free to contract with any other individual, no individual buyer or seller can say what the prevailing market value of a commodity will be. Instead, prices are determined by the market forces of supply and demand. If, as a seller, I ask for more than the prevailing market price, no one will buy from me. If, as a buyer, I offer less than the market price, no one will sell to me. In a system of competitive markets, prices are determined by the impersonal forces of supply and demand.

Smith calls prices determined by the forces of supply and demand operating in markets not affected by unnatural restrictions on free competition the "natural prices" of commodities. He contrasts such natural prices with the prices of commodities offered under conditions of monopoly, where one buyer controls the entire supply of a commodity: "The price of monopoly is upon every occasion the highest which can be got. The natural price, or the price of free competition, on the contrary, is the lowest which can be taken."[1] To be sure, a seller may, for a period of time, secure a price higher than that necessary to sustain the business. If, for example, an entrepreneur discovers a more efficient way to produce a commodity, then he or she can afford to produce the commodity for significantly less than the market price. At this point our entrepreneur has some discretion over how to price the product. The product cannot be priced above the market price, since then no one would buy it. Suppose then that the entrepreneur offers the product at the market price. In this case he or she will make higher-than-average profits. Alternatively, the entrepreneur can offer the product at below the market price, attempting to win buyers away from competitors. In either case, the market will adjust. If the product is sold at below the market price, competitors will have to adopt the more efficient methods of production in order to stay in business. If the product is sold at above-market price, entrepreneurs will be attracted into the industry by the higher-than-average profits, increasing the supply of the commodity and driving the price down. In either case, the price of the commodity will eventually fall to the lowest price sellers can afford to take and stay in business.

This example illustrates two important features of free markets. One feature is that competition provides every individual an incentive to produce more efficiently. Producers who can lower their costs of production can, at least temporarily, increase their profit margins. On the other hand, producers who are less efficient than their competitors will eventually be driven out of business. Because of the pervasive influence of this incentive to produce as efficiently as possible, a society that chooses to organize its economic life according to the principle of free competition will reap the greatest wealth possible from the resources available to it.

A second feature of free markets illustrated by our example is that they are self-regulating. Changes in production techniques, in the supply of raw materials, or in consumer preferences automatically induce changes in the quantity and kind of goods produced and in the prices of goods so as to achieve the most efficient use of resources possible. Individual buyers and sellers react to these changes, altering their behavior to maximize their own individual earnings. In so doing they alter the demand and supply of goods in the society as a whole. Without the intervention of any bureaucratic agency, the free market automatically adjusts the whole complex network of interconnected goods and services to achieve new equilibrium prices such that demand and supply of goods are in balance and no more efficient use of existing resources is possible. In the famous phrase of Adam Smith, free markets function as if guided by an "invisible hand" ensuring that the effort of each person to secure his or her own happiness is turned to the benefit of society as a whole.[2]

*The Wealth of Nations* is an extended argument for a system of free enterprise. At its most basic level, Smith's argument is that the best way for a nation to maximize its wealth is for it to adopt a system of free markets to govern its economic life. At the time Smith was writing, Britain's economic system was still marked by a variety of laws and regulations, many of them holdovers from the earlier feudal era, that in one way or another interfered with or prevented free competition in the production and sale of goods. Smith argued that it would be in the interest of the nation to do away with these laws and regulations, to adopt a system of free trade in which all governmental restrictions on commerce were removed.

*The Wealth of Nations* is a treatise in economic science. That is, it attempts to say how a system of free markets would in fact work and what the consequences of adopting such a system would be. In this sense *The Wealth of Nations* is fundamentally different in aim from the Declaration of Independence. The Declaration attempts to say how social life should be organized by appealing to laws of nature that prescribe how we should behave, even though we do not always actually behave in those ways. In contrast, *The Wealth of Nations* is primarily devoted to showing how a system of free markets would in fact invariably work out. Its primary content, the claims that free-market systems are efficient and self-regulating, is descriptive rather than prescriptive. Nonetheless, *The Wealth of Nations* does also have a prescriptive intent; Adam Smith clearly recommends free enterprise as an economic system that we should adopt. Let us turn now to a consideration of the prescriptive theory underlying Smith's recommendation.

## The Principle of Utility

In *The Wealth of Nations* Adam Smith argues that we should adopt a system of free markets to govern economic life. In fact, lurking in this "should" are two quite distinct standpoints: the standpoint of self-interest and the standpoint of morality. The difference between self-interest and morality is clear enough. If I say you should see a particular movie, most likely it is because I think you would enjoy it and that it is in your self-interest to do so. If I say you should keep your promise, most likely it is because I think you have a moral obligation to do so. Of course, we can imagine contexts in which I say you should see the movie for moral reasons. Perhaps, for example, I think the movie would convey to you the morally relevant suffering of people in some remote part of the world of which you were unaware. It is also possible that my recommendation that you keep your promise appeals to your self-interest rather than to morality. If, for example, you are in business and dependent upon repeat customers, it is in your self-interest to keep your promises to your customers. Nevertheless, there is a clear difference between the demands of self-interest and the demands of morality. My self-interest aims at my own well-being. Morality requires me to consider also the well-being of other people. The word *should* sometimes conveys a recommendation aimed at self-interest and sometimes conveys a recommendation aimed at morality.

If we ask whether Smith's recommendation that we should adopt a system of free markets to govern economic life aims at self-interest or morality, the answer is that it aims at both. The appeal to self-interest is clear enough. If we adopt a system of free markets, we will maximize the total amount of wealth produced by the nation. This will mean that there is more available for each of us. Now, of course some individuals will stand to lose from the adoption of a system of free markets—those individuals who benefit from governmental laws and regulations that prevent competition. Free enterprise is not in the self-interest of such individuals. It is, however, in the interest of the rest of us, who are not in a position to benefit from barriers to competition. Since most people are in this position, Smith's argument is that a system of free markets is in the self-interest of most people. However, because such a system would increase the total amount of wealth produced by the nation, it also would increase the amount of happiness in the nation as a whole. This fact, assuming here that Smith is right about this, is the foundation for a moral argument for free markets.

Suppose we adopt as a basic principle of morality the principle that we should maximize happiness. Suppose also that we are convinced by Adam Smith that a system of free markets would maximize happiness. Given these two suppositions, it follows that we (morally) should adopt a system of free markets. Our basic moral principle says that we should do whatever would maximize happiness, and Smith's economic science has shown us that a free-enterprise system would maximize happiness. It follows that such a system is morally desirable as well as desirable on grounds of self-interest.

The principle that we (morally) should do whatever maximizes happiness is known as the principle of utility, on the grounds that it recommends as the morally optimal course of action the one that is most useful to human beings, creatures who seek happiness. The philosophical theory that makes this principle the fundamental principle of ethics is known as utilitarianism. Although the utilitarian idea is suggested by Adam Smith, the English philosopher Jeremy Bentham was the first to clearly propose the principle as the single fundamental principle of morality. In 1789 Bentham, who considered himself a disciple of Adam Smith in economic theory, published his great work, *An Introduction to the Principles of Morals and Legislation.* In this work Bentham argued for the principle of utility as the single moral principle that should guide both individuals trying to decide what action to perform and legislators trying to decide what laws to enact.

## Utilitarianism and Rights

Bentham understood his utilitarian theory of morality as a radical alternative to the doctrine of natural law and natural rights. He rejected the whole idea of natural rights. Bentham viewed theories of natural law and natural rights, such as the one found in the American Declaration of Independence, as empty words devoid of any real content. In his view, claims to have certain rights made sense only if the rights claimed were legal rights derived from specific humanly made laws. Claims to such legal rights were clearly determinable, testable by appeal to the legislation creating them. On the other hand, claims about natural rights were not so clearly determinable. Is it obvious that all human beings are so equal by nature that none can claim a rightful authority over another? Is there any way, in principle, to resolve disputes about claimed natural rights? Bentham thought not. He regarded claims about natural rights as "metaphysical," like claims about how many angels can dance on the head of a pin.[3] He also regarded natural rights as unreal. A legal right, grounded in the humanly created legal system, is enforceable. In contrast, supposed natural rights are not enforceable. The American and French revolutionaries proclaimed a universal right to liberty, but even they admitted that for the most part, people were not in fact free. Slavery and tyranny were all too common. The supposed universal natural right to liberty was empty. Bentham's view is nicely summed up in his claim that "*natural rights* is simple nonsense," and that the "natural and imprescriptible rights" such as those claimed in the French Declaration of Rights are "nonsense upon stilts."[4]

In part, Bentham's hostility to the ideas of natural law and natural rights was a reaction to the use of those ideas to oppose change and reform. Bentham's fundamental aim was to persuade the English parliament to undertake a thoroughgoing reform of England's laws. In Bentham's view, the laws of England were profoundly warped to serve the interests of a privileged elite. Not surprisingly, many of the spokesmen for this privileged elite opposed the reforms championed by Bentham. These opponents of reform often defended their privileges as rights belonging to them by the laws of nature. Bentham regarded this defense as a subterfuge, one in which impressive but essentially empty words served "as a cloke, and pretence, and aliment, to despotism."[5] Having encountered such baseless appeals to natural law and natural rights, Bentham came to regard all such claims with disdain: "A great multitude of people are continually talking of the Law of Nature; and then they go on giving you their sentiments about what is right and what is wrong: and these sentiments, you are to understand, are so many chapters and sections of the Law of Nature."[6] In place of the morality of natural law and natural rights, Bentham thought that the principle of utility provided the foundation for a scientifically provable system of morality.

### Intrinsic and Extrinsic Value

To understand utilitarianism, it is helpful to draw a distinction between things that are intrinsically valuable and things that are extrinsically valuable. Things that are intrinsically valuable are things that are valuable in themselves. Things that are extrinsically valuable are things that are valuable as a means to something else. Money is a good example of something that is extrinsically but not intrinsically valuable. In itself it is only paper, or ordinary metals mixed with traces of gold or silver. What makes money valuable is that it is a means for acquiring other things we value—like food, clothing, shelter, or other goods. Truckloads of money would be of no value to a person stranded on an island with no way to use that money to acquire other goods.

If money has only extrinsic value, what things have intrinsic value? At first glance it looks as though food, clothing, and shelter would be things that are intrinsically valuable, since, unlike money, they appear to be valuable in themselves rather than for other things they can bring us. But is this always so? Shelter may be of no value in a tropical paradise, and clothing might be equally useless there. Even food can lack value in certain circumstances. A dying person may find swallowing, intravenous nutrition, and feeding tubes all painfully uncomfortable. For such a person food only prolongs suffering. Bentham argues that for human beings there are only two things that are intrinsically valuable: pain, which has negative intrinsic value, and pleasure, which has positive intrinsic value. The reason we value food is that normally it brings us pleasure—in the eating of it, in its capacity to bring an end to the pain of hunger, and in its capacity to sustain the life necessary for the enjoyment of other pleasures. When, as in the case of the dying patient, food brings only pain, it ceases to be valuable for us. What is desirable for us as human beings is to maximize happiness, to secure the most favorable balance of pleasure over pain that is possible for us to achieve. All other goods are valuable to us only extrinsically, as means to happiness.

## Utilitarianism and Egoism

It is important to distinguish utilitarian ethics from the ethics of egoism. The principle of ethical egoism is that each of us always should act to maximize his or her own happiness. From the point of view of ethical egoism, the happiness of other people should matter to me only insofar as their being happy makes me happy. If I am an egoist, only my own happiness is intrinsically valuable. It is my own happiness that I aim to maximize. In contrast, for a utilitarian ethics, the happiness of every person is intrinsically valuable. To act according to utilitarianism, I must calculate the expected effect of alternative acts upon the happiness of every person affected by those possible acts. I should then do the act that, among these possible acts, has the optimal outcome in terms of the total happiness produced. If a case should arise where performing a particular action maximizes the total amount of happiness possible in a group of people, even though performing that particular action makes me very unhappy, utilitarianism says that nonetheless, that particular action is what I should do. For example, suppose I can save the lives of many people, thereby creating great happiness, but I can do this only by sacrificing my own life. Ethical egoism would say that I should not sacrifice myself, while utilitarianism says that I should sacrifice myself. Egoism is selfish. Utilitarianism is not.

### Utilitarianism and Majoritarianism

It is also important to distinguish the principle of utilitarianism from the principle of majoritarianism. The majoritarian principle would say that the right thing to do is whatever the majority prefers. Often this will coincide with the course of action recommended by utilitarianism, since action preferred by the majority will make more people happy than any other action. However, the two principles do not always coincide. Suppose, for example, that doing X is preferred by a majority over doing Y. But suppose further that the members of the majority prefer X to Y by only a little bit while the members of the minority prefer Y to X by a great deal. In such a case it may turn out that doing Y would maximize total happiness, and thus be the course of action conforming to the principle of utility, while doing X would be the course of action conforming to the majoritarian principle.

In this example of the difference between utilitarianism and majoritarianism, the key thing is the different intensities of the preferences of the majority and the minority. The choice between X and Y makes a bigger difference to the members of the minority than it does to the members of the majority; the choice between X and Y has a more intense effect upon their happiness. Because of this difference in intensity, the selection of Y over X may maximize happiness even though X is preferred by a majority over Y.

### Utilitarianism as a Science of Morality

There are a number of other factors in addition to intensity that must be considered in evaluating alternative possible course of action from a utilitarian point of view. Duration is one such factor. Pleasures that last longer will contribute more to total happiness than pleasures that are of shorter duration. Probability is another factor that must be considered. Human action always takes place within a context of some uncertainty. One action might have a chance of producing a very great amount of happiness, while an alternative action might be likely to produce a somewhat lesser amount of happiness. However, if the greater happiness is, though possible, highly unlikely, while the lesser happiness is highly likely, then the aim of maximizing happiness may be best served by doing the act that aims at the lesser, though probable, payoff.

Bentham considers a number of factors that, like intensity, duration, and probability, should be considered in trying to determine which among the alternative possible actions would maximize the total amount of happiness produced. We need not consider each of these factors here. Each is a complicating consideration, but none of them affects the basic idea of the utilitarian approach: The right thing to do in any situation is whatever will maximize happiness. Bentham thought that this principle provides the foundation for a scientific approach to questions of morality. Confronted with a choice about what to do, the utilitarian principle gives us a formula for determining what is the morally correct thing to do. Having identified the possible actions before us, we have only to calculate, for each of these possible actions, the expected payoffs in terms of pleasure and pain, for each affected individual, of the performance of that possible action. Having determined these payoffs for each individual person, suitably refined by consideration of the durations, intensities, probabilities, and other variations of the pleasures and pains produced, we need only calculate from this data which among the alternative possible actions before us has the highest expected payoff in terms of the total happiness produced for society as a whole. From this point of view, questions of morality are decidable by the methods of social science and elementary arithmetic.

Of course, in practice this would not be an easy undertaking. In any real situation of choice we do not have the time to determine the happiness payoff for each affected person and probably could not determine the payoff for each with any degree of precision if we did have the time. Nonetheless, the ideal utilitarian calculus gives us a way of determining in principle what the morally right course of action is. Further, the utilitarian calculus can function as a regulative ideal. In practice we make a very rough estimate of the expected outcomes of the alternative possible actions before us, but this rough estimate is one that can be corrected by increased or more accurate information. The ideal calculus identifies the kinds of information that would be relevant to making such corrections. It may, as Bentham says, "always be kept in view."[7]

## Utilitarianism and the Common Rules of Morality

In practice, in the making of decisions in the everyday world, people are guided by a variety of moral rules. Among these rules are principles such as tell the truth, do not harm innocent people, pay your debts, help people in need, and a host of other familiar maxims. Bentham did not deny that these maxims were generally valid moral principles. But, he argued, it was because these principles are generally conducive to happiness that they are morally right. Thus, he argued, the principle of utility explains what it is that makes these maxims generally valid moral principles. The principle of utility is the single fundamental principle of morality. The maxims of ordinary moral life are applications of the principle of utility to common types of human interactions. Usually these maxims, if followed, do promote happiness. It is for this reason that they are generally valid moral principles. But sometimes these maxims do not hold. Truth telling, for example, is usually morally right, but most of us think that there are some cases when we should not tell the truth. So-called white lies are one sort of exception to the rule. The departing guest does the right thing in telling the host how much the evening was enjoyed even though the guest may have much preferred to have been elsewhere. To tell the truth on such an occasion would cause useless distress and unhappiness while the kindly lie causes happiness and does no harm. There are also occasions of a more serious nature when truth telling would not be the morally right course of action. Suppose, for example, that a male friend shows up one evening, enraged, drunk, waving a gun, and wanting to know where his girlfriend is. Should you tell him the truth? Surely not, since to do so risks great unhappiness. Bentham argues that it is one of the virtues of utilitarianism that it explains why we should not tell the truth in these cases. Such cases show that happiness is the deeper aim of morality and that the maxims of everyday moral life should be understood as rules of thumb that hold usually but not always. The ability of the principle of utility to explain why the principles of everyday morality were generally binding, and at the same time why they were not binding in some cases, provided a powerful argument in favor of Bentham's utilitarianism.

**Utilitarianism and the Politics of Reform**

In the early years of the nineteenth century, utilitarianism largely supplanted natural-rights theory as the dominant political philosophy of the English-speaking world. Presenting itself as a sober, scientific alternative to the revolutionary metaphysics of natural law, utilitarianism nonetheless provided a philosophical foundation for radical reforms of existing political institutions. In England, by the middle of the nineteenth century, the fundamental goals of the reform movement had coalesced into a coherent overall conception of how society should be organized. This is the conception of what is now known as classical liberalism. In the next chapter we will examine the fundamental features of classical liberalism and see how modern conservative thought emerged as a philosophical and political alternative to liberalism.

## Chapter 3

# Liberals and Conservatives

The period of transition from the eighteenth to the nineteenth century was a time of deep political change on both sides of the Atlantic Ocean. The American Revolution heralded the beginning of the end of European domination of the Americas and led to the formation of the first great republic of the modern era. The theories of natural law and natural rights that provided the moral justification for the revolution spread rapidly throughout the Americas, undermining the political legitimacy of the colonial system founded on the principle of the ruling prerogative of kings. In France, the doctrines of natural law and natural rights infused widespread discontent with the privileges, corruption, and incompetence of the king and the aristocracy, culminating in the revolutionary transformation of France's political system. In England, the intellectual homeland for both the Lockean theory of natural rights and the utilitarian philosophy of Jeremy Bentham, the new ideas simmered beneath the surface, threatening to explode the ruling order.

## Democracy and the Theory of Natural Rights

In late eighteenth-century England, wealth and power were firmly in the hands of a relatively small ruling elite. Though the power of the monarchy was checked by the power of an elected parliament, only a minority of the male population, those who owned substantial amounts of property, possessed the right to vote in parliamentary elections. Further, the distribution of seats in parliament, based on a hodgepodge of rights and privileges growing out of premodern conditions, gave overwhelmingly disproportionate power to those who held property in land and to those whose position in the dominant elite derived from England's precapitalist and preindustrial past.

The ideas of the American Revolution challenged this arrangement. Following Locke, the Americans argued that sovereignty, the ultimate legitimate ruling power within society, resided by natural law in the people themselves, and that governments were instituted among men to serve the people. When governments ceased to serve the people and became tyrants over them, the Americans claimed that natural law gave the people the right to overthrow the government and establish in its place a new government, one that would better serve the interests of the sovereign people.

These ideas of popular sovereignty and the right to revolution were derived from an account of governmental legitimacy found in the natural-law theory of John Locke. Lockean natural-law theory held that every human being had a right to liberty based in his nature as a being with the power of rational self-direction. Assuming that this is so, how is it that governments may legitimately pass laws that are binding upon the people? Are not all laws violations of the natural right to liberty possessed by each person? Lockean natural-law theory resolved this difficulty with its notion of a social contract. In a state of nature, with no government over them, every man would indeed possess the natural rights to life, liberty, and property; but, Locke argued, in a state of nature where no government existed, these rights are likely to be violated by other men. Consequently, it is in the interest of each to set up a government with police, courts, and jails to protect the natural rights of every individual. Accordingly, rational men in a state of nature would enter into a contract with one another to establish a government, each agreeing to abide by the laws of that government in exchange for the protection of individual rights provided by it.[1] However, when, by a long train of abuses of its legitimate powers, a government shows that it has ceased to serve the end of the social contract by which it is established, power reverts to the people who by their contract established that government.

In England these doctrines of popular sovereignty and the right to revolution grounded in it had largely disappeared from political discourse, appearing only in Whig historiography as legitimating grounds for the Glorious Revolution of 1688 that gave the English throne to William of Orange and established a parliamentary limit to royal power. Throughout most of the 1700s these doctrines remained safely located in the past. However, in the aftermath of the American and French Revolutions, these ghosts from the past came back to haunt England. Tom Paine, the English corset maker who served as a leading propagandist for the American Revolution, carried his revolutionary message to France and England as well. Back in England, in 1791 Paine published *The Rights of Man,* defending the French Revolution and attacking monarchy as inconsistent with human liberty. Other Englishmen similarly took the philosophy of the rights of man as the basis for a radical criticism of the English political system. Among these Englishmen were the philosopher and theologian Richard Price, the chemist Joseph Priestley, and Major John Cartwright, a former English naval officer who became the leader of a prodemocracy movement, demanding the right to vote for all adult English males. These radical ideas percolated downward in English society, reaching a host of artisans and skilled workmen who organized an array of unions and secret societies sympathetic to the ideas of natural law, natural rights, and popular sovereignty. Frightened, the English government cracked down. Meetings were banned. Publications were censured. Indicted for treason, Tom Paine fled to revolutionary France.

## Democracy and Utilitarianism

The radical challenge to England's political elite came from the revival of interest in the ideas of natural rights inspired by the American and French Revolutions. The founders of the utilitarian tradition, though reformers, were of a more conservative bent. We have already seen how Bentham dismissed the American ideas of natural law and natural rights as metaphysical nonsense. He also rejected the idea of the social contract as a fiction of no relevance to the real world.[2] Adam Smith was also critical of the American ideas.[3] David Hume, a protoutilitarian Scottish philosopher who influenced both Smith and Bentham, thought the American ideas to be patently absurd. The Americans claimed that according to the law of nature, sovereignty resided with the people and government rested upon the principle of social contract. Hume agreed with them that from this principle it did indeed follow that there should be "no taxation without representation." But, Hume argued, the principle of "no taxation without representation" was almost universally ignored. Everywhere governments taxed the ordinary people who had no say whatsoever about the making of the laws that governed them. Even in England, the country widely regarded as the freest in the world, parliament routinely taxed the common people, who had no right to vote. That the American principles implied that England, the freest country in the world, was not free was, in Hume's view, a clear sign of the absurdity of those principles.[4]

Hume's argument rested upon the assumption that England was fundamentally free and that, consequently, any principles implying otherwise must be mistaken. This argument would not appeal to radicals such as Paine or Price, who rejected Hume's assumption. However, other arguments were available to the utilitarians for resisting the demand for democracy. For the utilitarian, the merit of democracy would ultimately depend upon whether or not it was conducive to maximizing happiness for society as a whole. One might argue that the common people are not capable of wisely casting votes. If the common people are too shortsighted, too dense to see what measures will promote happiness, or too easily swayed by irrational appeals to emotion, then democratic institutions would not be conducive to maximizing the happiness of society as a whole. Adam Smith suggested such a view in his criticism of the Americans. Smith was alarmed at the "rancorous and virulent factions" that had appeared in the American states, and he suggested that the common people were likely to be carried away by irrational demands.[5] If this is true, to found a society on democratic principles would virtually guarantee its failure to promote the general happiness. It was easy for a utilitarian to see in the horrors of the Reign of Terror in France clear evidence of the propensity for "rancorous and virulent factions" to form among the people and of the likely social misery that follows therefrom. It was thinking along these lines that seemed to confirm Bentham in his resistance to the demand for democracy.[6] Nonetheless, there is nothing in utilitarianism that makes it in principle hostile to democracy. For the utilitarian, the question of whether or not democracy is morally and politically desirable depends upon whether or not, in fact, democracy promotes happiness.

If Bentham was not a revolutionary and radical democrat, he was nonetheless a reformer. In the late eighteenth century England's political system manifestly served the interests of a ruling elite. Worse from a utilitarian perspective, many of England's laws massively interfered with the pursuit of happiness of the many in order to achieve a small amount of happiness for the few. From the point of view of the principle of utility, which measured laws by their conduciveness to the greatest overall happiness, extensive legal reform was badly needed. However, Bentham's efforts at reform were consistently blocked. The ruling elite refused to make even the slightest concessions. Under these circumstances, Bentham and his followers began to rethink their position on democracy. As time passed it became apparent that without democracy, parliament would not reform the laws. Under the influence of his younger protégé, James Mill, Bentham came to advocate a limited form of democracy. In "Government," an article published in 1820, Mill presented the utilitarian argument for a democratic, representative form of government.[7] The argument clearly reflected the evolution of utilitarian thinking in England. Without a democratically representative government, Mill argued, the government would serve the interests only of the few, neglecting the interests of those excluded from the right to vote, and thereby failing to maximize happiness for the society as a whole. In order to get governmental policies to more nearly approximate the utilitarian idea of maximizing happiness, it would be necessary to extend the franchise to include a broader spectrum of the propertied and educated members of society. Reflecting earlier utilitarian fears about the ignorance and headstrong passions of the common people, Mill and Bentham continued to favor limiting the principle of democracy to exclude the common people from the right to vote, but it is clear how the principle of utility could be used to support even wider extensions of suffrage as it was, for example, in the hands of James Mill's son, John Stuart Mill. In *Considerations on Representative Government,* published in 1861, and *The Subjection of Women,* published in 1869 and coauthored with his wife, Harriet Taylor Mill, J.S. Mill argued on utilitarian grounds for further extensions of the franchise to include members of the working class and women, though it should be noted that he continued to favor a system of voting that would give greater weight to the educated elite.

## Free-Market Economics

In considering the issue of democracy, we have seen how distinct arguments for democracy could be developed from natural-law theory, on one hand, and from utilitarian theory, on the other. From the point of view of natural-law theory, the right of each citizen to have a vote in electing representatives was a requirement of the natural right to liberty inherent in every person. From the point of view of utilitarianism, democracy was morally right if it would maximize happiness and morally wrong if some alternative political system would produce a greater amount of happiness. By the middle of the nineteenth century, many of the leading utilitarian reformers had become convinced that greater democracy was necessary for the maximization of happiness. In this way utilitarians and natural-rights theorists could come to an agreement about the need for democracy despite the different reasons given by each camp in favor of democracy.

In a similar way, natural-rights theory and utilitarianism could each be seen as supporting the free-market economics of Adam Smith. As we have seen, for Smith himself, free markets were justified on utilitarian grounds, because they would work to maximize human happiness. However, it is also possible to argue for free markets from the point of view of natural-rights theory. After all, free markets are institutions within which buyers and sellers freely enter into agreements to exchange goods and services. Insofar as they act as free agents, human beings act in accordance with their natural right to liberty. Further, insofar as anyone or any government prevents the operation of free markets, they violate the natural right to liberty possessed by every human being to enter into voluntary agreements with other free agents. Hence it can be argued that only free-market economies are consistent with the natural right to liberty. Just as both utilitarianism and natural rights could be understood as supporting political democracy, so too both utilitarianism and natural rights could be understood as supporting free markets as the ideal institutional arrangement for the conduct of economic life.

## The Harm Principle

In *On Liberty,* published in 1859, the great utilitarian philosopher John Stuart Mill formulated a powerful principle designed to play a guiding role in all of political philosophy. This principle has come to be known as the harm principle.

> The object of this Essay is to assert one very simple principle, as entitled to govern absolutely the dealings of society with the individual in the way of compulsion and control, whether the means used be physical force in the form of legal penalties, or the moral coercion of public opinion. That principle is, that the sole end for which mankind are

warranted, individually or collectively, in interfering with the liberty of action of any of their number, is self-protection. That the only purpose for which power can be rightfully exercised over any member of a civilized community, against his will, is to prevent harm to others.[8]

The principle Mill here enunciates establishes a presumption in favor of individual liberty. It is only if an individual's action harms some other person that legal or social sanctions against it are permissible. It is not permissible to sanction actions because they are thought to be self-destructive, or because they are thought to be unwise, or because they are offensive to other people. In order for society to justly forbid some action, it must be shown to actually harm some other person. The harm principle thus provides the foundation for an entire theory of the proper role of all government and of all power exercised by society over the individual. Such power may be used to restrict the actions of an individual person only if the individual's action harms some other person. Acts of speech, written expression, assembly, worship, and contractual agreement for nonharmful purposes are beyond the reach of governmental or social control. According to the harm principle, the only just function of government is the protection of the liberty of individual citizens.

Mill himself argued for the harm principle on the basis of the principle of utility. He made the utilitarian foundation of his thinking quite clear: "It is proper to state that I forego any advantage which could be derived to my argument from the idea of abstract right, as a thing independent of utility. I regard utility as the ultimate appeal on all ethical questions."[9] Essentially Mill's argument was that, given the psychological makeup of human beings as creatures who find happiness in free action and unhappiness in restrictions on their freedom, societies conforming to the harm principle would maximize human happiness. Nonetheless, it is easy to see how a natural-rights theorist, who did embrace the idea of abstract right as a thing independent of utility, could also endorse the harm principle. For the natural-rights theorist, the harm principle appears to be a direct consequence of the natural right to liberty held by every human being. Thus again, as with the principle of democracy and the principle of free trade, the natural-rights theorist and the utilitarian could find common ground in the harm principle and the general conception of the proper role of governmental power based upon it.

## Classical Liberalism

By the middle of the nineteenth century a coherent vision of how society should be organized had taken shape in England, western Europe, and the Americas. This vision is the political ideology of classical liberalism. It is important not to confuse this classical liberalism with the political ideology known as "liberalism" in the United States in the twentieth century. In fact, the ideology of classical liberalism is closer to what today is a current of conservatism in the United States. Central to the classical liberalism of the nineteenth century is a commitment to the liberty of individual citizens. Freedom of religion, freedom of speech, freedom of the press, and freedom of assembly were core commitments of classical liberalism, as was the underlying conception of the proper role of just government as the protection of the liberties of individual citizens. Also central to classical liberalism was a commitment to a system of free markets as the best way to organize economic life. Political parties committed to these principles appeared in most of the countries on either side of the Atlantic Ocean. In England and many of the countries of western Europe and South America, these parties bore the name "Liberal." In the United States, where political parties were well established with other names, leading politicians within both the Republican and the Democratic parties expressed their commitment to the "liberal" principles of individual liberty and free markets.

Classical liberalism is a good example of a political ideology. A political ideology is a system of coherent and interconnected ideas that present a reasonably clear vision of how human social existence should be organized. A political ideology is a particular political philosophy. It brings together beliefs about human nature, beliefs about the findings of social science, beliefs about the likely consequences of particular policies, beliefs about moral values, and perhaps also beliefs about religion, history, and the meaning of human existence. Classical liberalism draws on the economic science of Adam Smith, the psychological insight into the importance of individual liberty to human beings, and the ethical theories of natural law and utilitarianism. While at their most abstract level utilitarianism and natural law disagree profoundly about what makes something morally right or wrong, when combined with convictions about the truth of Smith's economics and the psychology of human liberty, both theories agree in their endorsement of free markets and limited government. By the middle of the nineteenth century, convinced by the utilitarian critique of the idea of natural law, most philosophers had embraced the utilitarian philosophy. Nonetheless, being also convinced by Smith and Mill of the conduciveness to human happiness of maximal individual liberty, these same philosophers could warmly endorse the political principles championed by the natural-law theorists of the American and French Revolutions. The political ideology of classical liberalism, grounded in its twin commitments to individual liberty and free-market economics, became the overwhelmingly dominant political philosophy of the Atlantic world throughout the nineteenth century. As the century drew to a close, most classical liberals had also reluctantly followed Bentham and Mill into accepting the principle of democracy as well. Only governments elected by universal or near-universal suffrage could reasonably be expected to refrain from violating the liberty of their citizens in service to narrow interests, and only such governments could be expected to effectively promote the happiness of their citizens.

**The Idea of Progress**

There remains one other element that combined with the ideas already mentioned to form the political ideology of classical liberalism. This is the idea of progress. Perhaps no other name is more closely identified with the idea of progress than that of the Marquis de Condorcet, the French mathematician and philosopher. Born into the French aristocracy, as a young man Condorcet made a name for himself by publishing an essay on the calculus. In 1769, at the age of twenty-six, he was elected to the Academy of Sciences, where he soon assumed the position of secretary and the duty of that office of writing eulogies for members of the academy who had died. In this way Condorcet came to know the scientific contributions of the academicians and to have a sense for the progress of science.

Condorcet married the wealthy, beautiful, educated, and intelligent Sophie de Grouchy. Their home became one of the famous salons of prerevolutionary France, a center for philosophical, political, and artistic discussions involving important thinkers from France and overseas. Condorcet and his wife were strong supporters of the philosophy of natural rights. Tom Paine and Thomas Jefferson were among the intimates of the Condorcet household. When, following the French Revolution, Tom Paine was made a member of the French National

Assembly, Madame Condorcet served as his translator.[10] Adam Smith was also a friend of the Condorcets, and Condorcet was an admirer of Smith and a champion of free markets.[11]

When the French Revolution broke out, Condorcet was an enthusiastic spokesman for the revolutionary cause. He drafted a declaration of rights, based on the theory of natural rights.[12] As the revolutionaries divided into two camps—the moderate Girondins and the radical Jacobins—Condorcet tried to maintain an independent course. However, when the Jacobins gained the upper hand and expelled the Girondins, Condorcet wrote a scathing criticism of the constitution proposed by the Jacobins. On account of this, Jacobin leaders denounced Condorcet as an enemy of the revolution and ordered his arrest. The arrest order was issued on July 3, 1793. For the next nine months Condorcet was in hiding at the home of Madame Vernet, who risked her own safety to give him shelter. Hearing that the Jacobins had executed the leaders of the Girondins, Condorcet decided he must leave his shelter in order not to further expose Madame Vernet to danger. Having wandered about for several days, exhausted, Condorcet was captured and put in prison. The next morning, April 8, 1794, he was found dead in his prison cell. Whether his death was caused by poison administered by his own hand or by stress, exhaustion, and exposure is not clear.[13]

During the nine months that Condorcet was in hiding, he wrote his *Sketch of the Intellectual Progress of Mankind,* the work for which he is today best known. In the *Sketch* Condorcet presented a picture of human history as proceeding through a series of epochs. The ninth and culminating one of these epochs covered the period from the time of Descartes to the time of the French Revolution. The French mathematician, scientist, and philosopher René Descartes was one of the great minds of the seventeenth century. Along with Galileo, Kepler, and Newton, he was one of the champions of the Copernican revolution in astronomy and one of the giants of the new mathematical sciences. Along with many of his contemporaries, Condorcet saw in these new mathematical sciences the method by which human thought had escaped from the ignorance and superstition that had governed the epochs of the past. Despite his criticisms of the Jacobins, and despite the bloody guillotine that threatened his own life, Condorcet saw the French Revolution as the culmination of the struggle of the philosophers during the ninth epoch to apply the principles of science to questions of politics. In his eyes, the French Revolution was a giant step forward for humankind. Condorcet thought that, having freed itself from the shackles of ignorance and superstition, humanity was destined to march forever forward in time, ever progressing toward individual and social perfection. Henceforth, history would be the record of human progress. While it might be slow or fast, progress was inevitable. Retrogression was impossible. In the final chapter of the *Sketch,* devoted to the contemplation of the future, Condorcet wrote these words, words that surely must have reflected his own desperate circumstances:

> How consoling for the philosopher who laments the errors, the crimes, the injustices which still pollute the earth and of which he is often the victim is this view of the human race, emancipated from its shackles, released from the empire of fate and from that of the enemies it its progress, advancing with a firm and sure step along the path of truth, virtue and happiness![14]

Shortly after Condorcet's death, the National Assembly, which had itself ordered his arrest, arranged for the publication of his *Sketch of the Intellectual Progress of Mankind.* Condorcet's view of science, his optimistic faith in the power of human reason, and his conviction that history was progressive were widely shared by his contemporaries and by the nineteenth-century thinkers who came after him. The utilitarians, James Mill and John Stuart Mill, were influenced by him.[15] From Condorcet and many others the idea of progress as the fate for which humankind was surely destined became yet another of the ideas that made up the political ideology of classical liberalism.

## The Origins of Conservative Thought

Not everyone shared Condorcet's enthusiasm for the French Revolution. Condorcet's optimistic assessment of it, and his confidence in the progressive course of history, rested on a faith in the power of human reason. Condorcet was inspired by the successful application of human thought to the problems of understanding the natural world. He saw in the origins of modern science, and the underlying scientific method, the key to the solutions of the problems of social and political life. By the application of human reason, he thought, these problems could be solved. A similar confidence in the power of human reason to solve the fundamental problems of politics was shared by both the natural-rights theorists and the utilitarians. For the natural-rights theorists, the laws of nature, from which natural rights could be derived, were discoverable by reason. They were, indeed, often called the laws of reason. Similarly, the extensive program of reform championed by Bentham and his followers was, in their view, based on a genuine science, the moral science constituted by the utilitarian calculus. A faith in the capacity for human beings to rationally reconstruct the laws and institutions of social life, to reform and improve upon the ways of the past, was built into the fabric of classical liberalism. In *Reflections on the Revolution in France,* published in 1790, Edmund Burke called this faith into question. In doing so, he laid the foundations for modern conservative thought.

Two thoughts are central to Burke's reflections: a sense of the limitations of human reason, and a sense of the wisdom of the past. Classical liberals such as Condorcet saw the past as a record of folly, ignorance, and superstition. They looked upon the laws and institutions of their times as products of this past folly. The revolutionaries in France and the radical reformers among the Benthamites were equally ready to sweep aside the laws and institutions of the past and to replace them with laws and institutions of their own making. Burke saw in this a folly more profound and more dangerous than anything received from the past. The laws and institutions received from the past had emerged little by little in response to diverse practical needs. They had served the generations of the past and been handed down to the present from those generations. This very fact was evidence that these laws and institutions were not so bad after all. In a sense, their very survival proved their fitness as rules for governing human life. Now the reformers and the revolutionaries wanted to do away with these proven traditions. Unable themselves to see the wisdom of the past, they sought to tear it all down and replace it with a new vision of their own. But, Burke argued, the reformers and the revolutionaries overestimated their own powers of reason. If they could not see the wisdom of the past, it was not because there was no wisdom there, but rather because the reformers and revolutionaries were insufficiently wise to see it. And if they thought they could create a better world by building on the blueprints of their own thoughts, they confused wisdom with idle fantasy. At the heart of liberalism, Burke saw a hubristic overestimation of the power of human reason, a dangerous folly that threatened to bring disaster upon the heads of all. For Burke, the rabid factions, political violence, and chaos that followed the French Revolution were the consequences of this dangerous folly. For him the bloody guillotine was no surprise.

A second criticism of classical liberalism comes from *An Essay on the Principle of Population,* written by Thomas Malthus and published in 1798. Malthus offered his essay as an explicit reply to Condorcet and others who claimed that progress could overcome the social conditions of misery and distress. Malthus argued that human populations had a natural tendency to increase at an exponential rate while the supply of food increased only at an arithmetical rate. The consequence of these natural tendencies was to keep the level of population constantly pushing against the available means of subsistence. As a result, poverty and unmet needs were unavoidable features of human life. Though war, famine, and disease might temporarily reduce human population to manageable levels, the natural tendency for exponential growth in population would soon restore conditions of poverty and social distress. Where Burke had challenged the faith in the power of human reason underlying classical liberalism, Malthus denied the very possibility of progress, at least as understood by Condorcet and others, as the gradual achievement of a social state within which poverty and other conditions of social distress would be overcome.

A third criticism of classical liberalism is less easy to summarize but is also constitutive of an important thread in conservative thought. For the classical liberals, whether rooted in the theory of natural rights or rooted in the theory of utilitarianism, individual human beings were understood as the fundamental units of social and political life. For the natural-rights theorist, individual people were autonomous self-governing agents, surrounded by a protective shield of natural rights. For the utilitarian, social relationships between human beings were valuable only insofar as the individuals involved derived pleasure from those relationships. In the new world order emerging on both sides of the Atlantic at the dawn of the nineteenth century, these individuals were liberated from the traditional ties of religion, class, and place that defined who a person was in the social systems of the past. In the emerging systems of legal rights, representative government, and free-market economics, people entered into relationships with one another solely as agents freely contracting in pursuit of their own happiness. They were free, but they were also on their own.

If classical liberals found liberty and happiness in this new world order, others found in it a profound loneliness. They described the world embraced by classical liberalism as an impoverished, dehumanized world. Conservatives saw that a world in which religious traditions, moral conventions, and social hierarchies bound each person in a thick and nurturing system of human relationships had given way to a world in which ties between human beings had been reduced to relationships of mutual use. In the nineteenth century these themes were developed by poets and essayists who looked back with some regret on the world left behind and ahead with some trepidation to the world of the future. Among those who voiced these concerns were the poet and novelist Sir Walter Scott, the poet and essayist Samuel Taylor Coleridge, and the social critics Thomas Carlyle and John Ruskin. In their work, with varying emphases, there emerged the contrast between a humane past and an alienated present, a theme that would become common in future political philosophy.

A fourth element of conservative thought concerned respect for traditional religious teachings and the importance of Christianity as a foundation for society. Rooted in the Enlightenment critique of superstition, classical liberalism looked upon traditional Christianity as a system of superstition inimical to human progress. If not openly atheistic, liberals were apt to be followers of systems of natural religion that discarded the biblical foundations of Christianity and attempted to place religion on a foundation of natural science. Conservatives resisted this abandonment of traditional Christianity, believing in the more or less literal truth of the Bible and the continued value of Christian doctrine and the Christian church as foundations for social life. They also rejected the utilitarian view that human happiness was the ultimate goal, believing that our fundamental duties were to God and that, in a sense, we belonged to God rather than to ourselves.

Though less tightly organized into a system of interlocking ideas, these four themes—the dangerous folly of utopian faith in human reason, the impossibility of the elimination of human misery, the alienating conditions of life championed by classical liberalism, and the continued relevance of Christianity—appeared in response to the emerging ideology of classical liberalism. Together they constitute the core ideas of a conservative alternative to classical liberalism. This conservative ideology would remain and develop as a coherent political alternative to classical liberalism in political philosophy.

# —— Chapter 4 ——

# Anarchists and Socialists

One of the central features of classical liberalism was a commitment to the economic theory of laissez-faire capitalism. Though, as we have seen, one could come to support the free-market theories of Adam Smith on the basis of the theory of natural rights, it was the utilitarian argument that generally prevailed throughout most of the nineteenth century. The utilitarian argument, stressing the beneficial consequences of free markets, was the argument advanced by Smith himself and, with the general ascendancy of utilitarianism over natural-rights theory throughout the nineteenth century, it was the utilitarian argument most often cited in support of free-market economics.

At the heart of this utilitarian argument was the idea that free markets would deliver the goods. Adam Smith argued that the best way to advance the wealth of a nation was to organize its economic life according to the principles of free trade. Though aware of the need for governmental authority to be on guard against the attempts of entrepreneurs to monopolize markets or prevent competition, Smith claimed that truly free markets would, in the long run, benefit nearly everyone. With an increase in the overall wealth of the nation, the portion falling to each individual would grow. In the long run, ordinary working men and women would be better off than they would be under any alternative economic system.

By the middle of the nineteenth century, this optimistic prognosis seemed to be contradicted by the grim realities of the new capitalist order. To be sure, the young capitalist system had produced astonishing wealth in a very short period of time. In England, parts of continental Europe, and parts of the Americas, mines, factories, canals, and railroads had been built. Great cities devoted to manufacturing, trade, and commerce appeared in what just decades before had been a largely rural landscape. But, at the same time, the new system had produced a world of squalor and grinding poverty. This world was inhabited by the newly created working class, a class of people who lived by selling their labor power to the owners of the mines and factories of the emerging industrial world. The men, women, and children of this working class labored fourteen, sixteen, and even eighteen hours per day, six days per week, in places that were dangerous, poorly lit, and polluted by dust and fibers that filled the air. For this they received wages barely sufficient to pay for meager food and for crowded rooms in the urban slums that grew up in the new industrial towns. Family life deteriorated. Children grew up unchurched and unschooled. Men and women turned to the consolations of alcohol and drugs. Begging, vagabondage, prostitution, and crime became familiar aspects of working-class life. Respiratory diseases caused by the polluted and crowded conditions brought many to an early death. This is the world depicted in the novels of Charles Dickens.[1] It was a world of wealth and poverty standing side by side, divided by the fences of private property. Accordingly, it is not surprising that questions about the rights of private property came to play a central role in the political philosophy of the nineteenth century.

## Property Rights

To hold a thing as a piece of property is to have a bundle of rights with respect to that thing. The owner of a piece of land has the right to use that land, the right to exclude other people from using the land, the right to sell the land, the right to bequeath the land, and the right to give the land away. It is possible for an individual to hold one or more of these rights without holding all of them. For example, in England and much of Europe, private property in land was often restricted. The system of entailment stipulated the succession of heirs to a landed estate, in effect removing the right of bequeathment from the bundle of rights held by the owner of the land. Medieval law and tradition sometimes also recognized the right of peasants to forage for firewood on the estates of their feudal lords, thereby limiting the right of exclusive use belonging to the owner of the land. As the new capitalist order emerged from the feudal past, owners of property sought to remove these restrictions and secure full property rights over land, rights like those held by the new capitalist class with its wealth in industrial and commercial property. For the most part, owners of property were successful in this, and by the end of the nineteenth century nearly all of the land, mines, forests, factories, means of transportation, and means of communication were privately owned. The owners of these productive resources, the capitalists, formed a relatively small portion of the population, with the vast majority of men and women belonging to the working class, a class of individuals who owned no productive resources and who made their living by selling their labor power to the capitalists who did own these things. Ownership of such private property brought wealth. For those who lacked such property, poverty and its attendant miseries was a constant threat.

### Natural Rights and Property Rights

As legal rights, property rights are clearly human creations, but are there any natural moral rights to private property? On the face of it, it might seem that there are not. After all, how could a person come to have, by nature, rights over some particular piece of land or some particular object? People normally acquire property by purchase, bequeathment, or gift. But each of these means presupposes a prior right of property belonging to the person who sells, bequeaths, or gives away whatever piece of property it might be. To account for a natural right of ownership of the one who acquires property formerly belonging to another, it will be necessary to give some kind of account of how natural rights of property can originally be acquired in some object. How is it that human beings, finding themselves on the face of the earth either by the hand of God or by some process of evolution, come to have a right over some portion of the earth or some object on it?

In his *Second Treatise of Government,* John Locke attempts to provide an account of original acquisition by which a person can come to have a natural right of ownership over some piece of land or some object even though originally God has given all things to men in common. Locke says this:

> Though the Earth, and all inferior Creatures be common to all Men, yet every Man has a *Property* in his own *Person.* This no Body has any Right to but himself. The *Labour* of his Body, and the *Work* of his

Hands, we may say, are properly his. Whatsoever then he removes out of the State that Nature hath provided, and left it in, he hath mixed his *Labour* with, and joyned to it something that is his own, and thereby makes it his *Property*. It being by him removed from the common state Nature placed it in, hath by this *labour* something annexed to it, that excludes the common right of other Men. *Labour* being the unquestionable Property of the Labourer, no Man but he can have a right to what that is once joyned to, at least where there is enough, and as good left in common for others.[2]

In this famous passage, Locke provides an account of how a piece of property belonging in common to all human beings legitimately could come to be the private property of some individual person. At the center of Locke's account is the idea that every person has a natural right over his or her own labor and that it is by mixing labor with something in its natural state that a person comes to ownership rights over property. Assuredly, there are some odd features to this account. If a man plows some previously uncultivated soil, mixing his labor with it, just how much land does he thereby acquire? Does he gain rights to minerals far below the surface?[3] However, for now at least, we will set this difficulty aside and assume that Locke has succeeded in providing a tenable account of how legitimate rights over property might be acquired and consequently also how legitimate rights over property might come to be held by purchase, bequeathment, or gift. Still, some interesting difficulties remain.

### The Anarchist Critique of Private Property

In 1840 Pierre-Joseph Proudhon, son of a cooper and himself a printer by trade, published a book entitled *What Is Property?* Proudhon answered this question in a single word: "theft." His argument was simple. If one traces actual ownership claims backward in time, Proudhon argued, one eventually comes to a point of origin, and that point of origin in fact invariably rests upon an act of force in which some individual claimed something as exclusively his own and by force excluded others from their common right of use. Since this is so, and since violent exclusion of others from the use of that to which they have a right is an act of theft, it follows that all original claims of property ownership rest on a primitive act of theft and are therefore illegitimate. Of course, it also follows that all subsequent rights over property, based on transfer by sale, bequeathment, or gift from those original violent seizures, are also illegitimate, since the person who transferred the property to another never had a legitimate title in the first place.

## Anarchism

Proudhon was a revolutionary anarchist. He viewed all coercive power over human beings as a violation of their natural right to liberty. The exclusive claims of private property, grounded in original acts of violence and backed up by the coercive power of law, became the means by which peasants and workers were crushed and oppressed. The state and the whole system of law were at bottom nothing more than instruments of oppression, incompatible with the natural liberty of human beings. "To be GOVERNED," said Proudhon, "is to be watched, inspected, spied upon, directed, law-driven, numbered, regulated, enrolled, indoctrinated, preached at, controlled, checked, estimated, valued, censured, commanded, by creatures who have neither the right nor the wisdom nor the virtue to do so."[4] In place of the coercive principles of law and the state, Proudhon proposed a revolutionary reorganization of the whole of society, based upon the principle of contracts mutually agreed upon by all parties. The illegitimate ownership rights claimed by the capitalists who controlled the land, mines, and factories were to be swept aside, and these productive resources be given over in common to the control of the workers who labored in them.

## The Ricardian Socialists

There is a curious passage in *The Second Treatise*. Having introduced the idea that it is by mixing labor with a part of nature that one comes to have a right over that part of nature, Locke goes on to say, "Thus the Grass my Horse has bit; the Turfs my Servant has cut; and the Ore I have digg'd . . . become my *Property*."[5] Now, leaving the horse aside, why is it that the turfs Locke's servant cut come to belong to Locke and not to the servant? By nature, surely, it is to the servant they belong.

The idea that the by natural right the fruits of labor belong to the laborer serves as one of the premises for a simple but powerful argument for the conclusion that capitalism was unjust. The other premise upon which this argument rests comes from the science of economics created by Adam Smith and developed by Smith's successor, David Ricardo. According to Smith and Ricardo, the value of a thing is proportional to the amount of labor necessary to produce it.[6] This idea, known as the labor theory of value, reduces the value of all things to the labor contained in them. Smith and Ricardo used the labor theory of value to explain the relative exchange rates of commodities: why a pair of shoes cost as much as two shirts, for example. But in the 1820s certain critics of capitalism combined Ricardo's labor theory of value with Locke's labor theory of property rights to produce a simple but powerful argument against capitalism. According to Locke's principle, the laborer had a right of ownership in the products of his labor. According to Ricardo's labor theory of value, the value of all commodities was a product of the labor necessary to produce them. From these two premises it followed that everything should belong to the laborers. But in the capitalist system it was the capitalist, the owner of the factory who employed the laborer, who claimed the product of the laborer as his own. This, the Ricardian socialists argued, was an injustice inherent in the very nature of the capitalist system of production.[7]

Although they possessed a clear and powerful argument that capitalism was unjust, the Ricardian socialists were less clear about how society ought to be organized. They did, however, contribute to a number of experiments aimed at establishing islands of justice in the sea of supposedly unjust capitalism. Labor exchanges were organized, in which craftsmen could bring the objects they had produced and exchange them for other objects of equal labor value. More ambitious projects aimed at establishing whole alternative communities, separated from the surrounding capitalist system, and organized on the principle of reward according to the amount of labor performed.

## Christian Socialism

Other utopian communities were organized on the basis of the principles of Christianity. Etienne Cabet, a French Christian socialist and author of the popular utopian novel *Voyage to Icaria,* inspired the foundation of a number of communist communities, most of them located in the New World, where land was plentiful and cheap.

Cabet blamed the social problems of his time on greed. He preached an austere ethic of the renunciation of desire and diversity. All property was to be owned by the community as a whole, and each member was to receive equal food, clothing, and shelter. Where the Ricardian socialists had appealed to the principles of Locke and Adam Smith to justify their socialist ideas, Cabet claimed to base his ideas on the commandments of God as revealed by Jesus Christ. After all, did not Christ tell the rich young man to give away all that he had to the poor? And does not scripture tell us that the disciples of Christ practiced communism?

> Now the company of those who believed were of one heart and soul, and no one said that any of the things which he possessed was his own, but they had everything in common. . . . There was not a needy person among them, for as many as were possessors of lands or houses sold them, and brought the proceeds of what was sold and laid it at the apostles' feet, and distribution was made to each as any had need.[8]

Here in the principles of the early Christian community, Cabet and thousands of other Christians found the basis for a communal way of life radically different from the individualistic quest for wealth at the heart of capitalism.

## The Socialism of Marx and Engels

When the *Manifesto of the Communist Party* appeared in the spring of 1848, Karl Marx and Frederick Engels were obscure German socialists living in exile in London. By the end of the nineteenth century their ideas had come to dominate the radical labor movement aimed at the overthrow of capitalism. In the twentieth century their ideas inspired the creation of Communist states in Russia, Eastern Europe, China, and elsewhere.

At the center of Marxist thought was Marx's theory of capitalism. Marx began this work in the mid-1840s. An unpublished draft of his theory, now known as the *Grundrisse*, was written during the winter of 1857–58. A second version of the theory was published in 1859 under the title *Contribution to the Critique of Political Economy*. A third version appeared in 1867 with the publication of the first volume of *Capital*, a projected multivolume study of capitalism. (Only that one volume had been actually published by the time of Marx's death in 1883.) Despite its unfinished nature, this work on capitalism, occupying nearly forty years, filling several thousand pages of text, and informing all of his other works, was the major theoretical achievement of Marx's lifetime.

In many ways Marx shared the theoretical outlook of the classical economists Adam Smith and David Ricardo. Like Smith and Ricardo, he sought to analyze the workings of a capitalist system characterized by free markets and private ownership of the means of production. Like his classical predecessors, he used the labor theory of value, according to which the value of a commodity was determined by the amount of labor necessary to produce it, as the basis for a theory of relative prices of commodities and for a theory of the relative shares of total wealth going to the owners of land, labor, and capital. And, like Smith and Ricardo, Marx was tremendously impressed with the productive powers of capitalism:

> The bourgeoisie [the class of capitalists], during its rule of scarce one hundred years, has created more massive and more colossal productive forces than have all preceding generations together. Subjection of Nature's forces to man, machinery, application of chemistry to industry and agriculture, steam-navigation, railways, electric telegraphs, clearing of whole continents for cultivation, canalization of rivers, whole populations conjured out of the ground—what earlier century had even a presentiment that such productive forces slumbered in the lap of social labour?[9]

Nonetheless, unlike Smith and Ricardo, Marx was also highly critical of capitalism.

In *The Wealth of Nations,* Adam Smith argued that capitalism would benefit the vast majority of the population. The invisible hand of the free market would yoke the self-interest of each agent to the cause of increasing the total wealth produced, thereby increasing the share available to each individual person. Smith offered an optimistic prognosis for the future of capitalism, foreseeing peaceful competition, a steady increase in the production of goods and services, and a steady increase in the share of those goods and services going to everyone willing to put his hands or head to work.

Marx argued that this optimistic prognosis rested upon important errors in Smith's economic theory. Marx's own theory of capitalism offered a pessimistic prognosis. Though he agreed with Smith about the productive power inherent in capitalism, Marx's economic theory differed from Smith's theory about the likely effects of capitalism on the lives of ordinary people. Marx saw capitalism as a "contradictory" social system. As capitalism developed over time, it did produce greater and greater productive forces. But it also produced a greater and greater concentration of wealth. In the competitive world of free markets, successful firms grew larger and larger, gradually eliminating their less successful rivals. Competition gave way to monopoly. The vast productive power produced by capitalism gradually came under the control of fewer and fewer people. Over time, the bourgeoisie, the class of capitalists, those who owned the means of production, became smaller, and the proletariat, the class of workers, those who owned no land, mines, or factories and lived by the sale of their labor power, grew larger. Marx also argued that over time, as the new productive machinery produced by capitalism displaced human labor, capitalism resulted in an ever-growing pool of unemployed workers. Faced with intense competition, each individual capitalist was forced to reduce the costs of production as much as possible. Wherever possible, the capitalist sought to replace human labor with the less expensive labor of machines. Wherever human labor remained necessary, the capitalist sought to increase the output and reduce the costs of that labor as much as possible. With increasing numbers of unemployed workers competing for jobs, workers were forced to take jobs that provided little pay and demanded long and arduous effort. The working class, far from benefiting from the increased powers of production produced by capitalism, found itself riveted to drudgery and poverty.

There was also a historical dimension to Marx's theory of capitalism that was missing from the economic theory of Adam Smith. Smith conceived of capitalism as involving a system of competitive markets. He thought of this competitive system as stable, persisting over time as capitalism grew and developed. Marx, however, saw the system of competition as inherently unstable. In the sea of competition, the big fish eat the little fish. Over time, markets come to be dominated by a few large firms that exercise monopolistic or oligopolistic control. The class structure that is fundamental to capitalism also changes over time. Gradually the small capitalists are eliminated, falling prey to larger and stronger capitalists, who are better able to finance investment in more productive new technologies and better able to withstand the stresses produced by hard times. As capitalism develops, wealth and power come to be concentrated in the hands of a very few, and the vast majority are reduced to the role of impoverished wage laborers. Where Adam Smith saw capitalism as a stable system, gradually reproducing itself on a grander and grander scale, Marx saw capitalism as inherently unstable, gradually transforming itself, by its own innate logic, into something quite different from the competitive system of free producers envisaged by Adam Smith.

This historical dimension to Marx's conception of capitalism finds a place in a broader understanding of history suggested by Marx in a number of places. Marx sees capitalism as a distinctive form of life. In his view, capitalism emerges at a particular moment in history, evolves in the ways suggested above, and eventually will pass away. Marx saw capitalism as emerging out of feudalism in western Europe in the sixteenth and seventeenth centuries. He held that capitalism would grow and expand to all corners of the globe, gradually transforming itself into ever more concentrated forms of wealth as it did so. Marx also predicted that eventually the working class would come to see that capitalism was inimical to its interests, would organize itself into a revolutionary agent for change, and would overthrow capitalism, replacing it with a system of socialism.[10]

Marx had relatively little to say about what this system of socialism would be like. He seems to have thought of a decisive battle for political power and control of the state between workers and capitalists. After the victory of the working class, there would follow a transition period of indeterminate length during which the working class would use its control of the state to pass laws that would, step by step, transform monopolistic capitalism into a fully socialist form of social organization. Fully developed socialism would involve the collective and democratic ownership and control of the means of production, would operate according to the maxim "From each according to his ability and to each according to his need," and would provide the conditions necessary "for the free development of all."[11]

Despite their sketchy nature, Marx's descriptions of socialism are sufficiently outlined to make clear important differences between the Marxist vision and the visions of the future advanced by other socialists and by the anarchists. Nineteenth-century socialists such as Robert Owen, Etienne Cabet, and Charles Fourier saw socialism as emerging through the formation of experimental communities by the voluntary association of like-minded persons. These communities would first exist as islands of socialism within the sea of capitalism. It was hoped that these socialist communities would demonstrate to all that socialism was better for human beings than capitalism and that, having seen the proof of socialism, more and more people would join together to create a network of communal societies so vast that it would eventually displace capitalism as the dominant form of social organization.

Marx and Engels viewed this vision as utopian. The productive powers created by capitalism could not be utilized in a society consisting of such communities. Railroads, canals, and telegraph lines spanned vast geographic distances and, even in the nineteenth century, trade had taken on truly global dimensions. How were these resources to be managed in the society of the future? Marx and Engels were convinced that the conditions necessary for the free development of all presupposed the ability to effectively use the productive powers created by capitalism for the good of all human beings. But to effectively manage the productive resources created by capitalism, the socialist society of the future would require national and even international forms of cooperation. For the Marxists, gaining control of the political power of the nation-state was critical for creating the forms of cooperation necessary for the socialist society of the future. This emphasis on the importance of obtaining control of the political apparatus of the state also distinguished the Marxists from the anarchists. The Marxists contended that it was only by obtaining political control of the state that the working class could gain the means by which the socialist society of the future could be created. The anarchists, convinced that all forms of the state were inimical to individual liberty, viewed the Marxists with suspicion. They feared that the Marxian brand of socialism would only increase the oppressive powers of the state.

Like the anarchists and like all socialists, Marxists viewed the reign of capitalist private property as oppressive to the vast majority of humankind. It is in their conception of capitalism as a necessarily transient form of life embedded within a larger process of historical development, and in their conception of the role to be played in the creation of a more humane world by working-class control of the state, that Marxists differed from other socialist and anarchist critics of capitalism. In the closing decades of the nineteenth century this Marxist understanding of capitalism and the way to its overcoming came to dominate the growing movement of the working class, a movement that called for the revolutionary transformation of the whole social system.

## The Ideology of Socialism

The Marxist variant that came to dominate the socialist movement late in the nineteenth century formed an ideological alternative to both conservatism and classical liberalism. In several important respects, socialist ideology shared key ideas with the ideology of classical liberalism. Like classical liberalism, socialist ideology appealed to the ethical norms of freedom and human happiness. It also placed a great deal of faith in the power of human reason to understand human social existence and, on the basis of this understanding, construct a social system radically different from the social systems of the past. Also like classical liberalism, socialist ideology was generally optimistic about the course of history, believing in not only the possibility but also the actuality of a generally progressive direction to the historical process. The chief point of contention between socialist and classical liberal ideologies pertains to the assessment of the likely consequences of capitalism as a way of life. Where classical liberals were optimistic, expecting the growth of total production produced by capitalism to benefit the vast majority of people, socialists were pessimistic, expecting the growth of total production produced by capitalism not to benefit the vast majority of people. It is important to see that this central point of disagreement concerns a question of social science: What would be the long-term consequences of capitalism? In terms of its underlying ethical values, socialist ideology shares the values of the liberal tradition.

Socialist ideology has less in common with conservative ideology. It rejects conservative beliefs in the wisdom of tradition and the dangers of radical change. It also rejects conservative religious views that subordinate the human ends of freedom and happiness to transcendent ends and purposes. Socialists do agree with conservatives about the alienated character of human existence within a capitalist mode of production. Like conservatives, socialists deplore the dehumanization resulting from the supposed capitalist reduction of all human relationships to relationships of mutual use. However, where conservatives looked for at least a partial restoration of pre-capitalist restraints on the forces of the free market, socialists looked forward to the abolition of capitalism and its replacement with socialist forms of life based on humane relationships grounded in democracy and solidarity among people. On the whole, then, socialist ideology is much closer to the humanistic, rationalistic, and optimistic outlook of classical liberalism than it is to the divine-centered, traditionalist, and cautious outlook of conservative ideology.

## Socialism and Communism

In the *Manifesto,* Marx and Engels conclude a brief overview of the course of capitalist development with a prediction of a class war "where the violent overthrow of the bourgeoisie lays the foundation for the sway of the proletariat."[12] These words were published in the spring of 1848, at a time of acute economic and political crisis within the capitalist world of England and western Europe. At the time they were written, the working class lacked the right to vote. Violent rebellion seemed to be the only avenue for change. Decades later, with the male working class having gained at least in part the right to vote in several European countries, Marx allowed that, where the working class did have the right to vote, the revolutionary overthrow of the bourgeoisie might be achieved by peaceful means.[13]

Marx's recognition of a possible peaceful path to socialism is significant in at least two respects. First, it indicates the important point that the Marxist idea of a revolution should not be confused with the idea of violent change. Marx conceived of the transition from capitalism to socialism as revolutionary because it constituted a fundamental change in the way social life was to be organized. Whether this revolutionary change was to be violent or peaceful was a separate issue. Second, with the extension of the right to vote to much of the male working class in various European countries in the last quarter of the nineteenth century, socialists of the decades after the deaths of Marx and Engels, even those who considered themselves orthodox Marxists, almost uniformly embraced the peaceful, electoral path to socialism. Social Democratic political parties appeared in most European countries, claiming to be guided by the "scientific socialism" of Marx and Engels and pinning their hopes for the future on the votes of their working-class followers.

In Russia things were different. Russia, and the greater Russian

Empire, were ruled by an autocratic monarch, the tsar. In Russia there was no elected parliament, and freedom of speech, freedom of the press, and freedom of assembly were severely truncated. The Social Democratic party was illegal in Russia, and spies and police agents infiltrated the party at every level, reporting party activities and party members to the tsar's agents. Union organizers and Social Democratic activists were arrested and deported to Siberia. Under these conditions it was suicidal to attempt to emulate the Social Democratic parties of western Europe, developed to follow the electoral path to socialism. Responding to the repressive and backward conditions found in Russia, V.I. Lenin proposed a "party of the new type," made up of committed revolutionaries. The party would be a secret organization, with membership at each level known only to those party functionaries necessary to coordinate the activities of the party. The party would be organized according to the principles of democratic centralism. Whenever the party was faced with an important issue, there was to be democratic debate among members of the party about what action should be taken. This debate would occur at whatever level was necessary to deal with the issue and would often take place in secret meetings of small groups or in large meetings outside the borders of Russia and beyond the repressive control of the tsar's agents. Once a decision was reached by democratic vote, all members of the party were to be bound to obey the decision reached. The party was also to be hierarchically organized, with decisions reached at the highest levels being binding on party members at all lower levels. Lenin proposed such a party structure as a way of making maximally effective use of revolutionary activists under conditions of tsarist repression. He advanced his proposal for a new type of party in *What Is to Be Done?* in 1902.[14] One year later, at a congress of the Russian Social Democratic Labor Party in London, the majority, or Bolshevik, faction of the party adopted Lenin's proposals, creating a Marxist, secret, disciplined, and highly centralized revolutionary party. Until World War I, this Leninist form of party organization was largely unknown outside Russia. However, the war and the events that followed the war would change this.

For Marxists around the world, World War I was no surprise. Marxian socialists had predicted the war and had long debated how the working-class parties should respond to it. At international conferences in Stuttgart in 1907 and Basel in 1913, Social Democrats pledged to work against war and to push for revolutionary change in the event that war broke out. When war did come, the great Social Democratic parties of Germany and western Europe betrayed these commitments, fearing to make the revolutionary attempt. But in Russia the Bolsheviks did lead a successful revolutionary attempt, seizing power and successfully holding that power through the course of a long and terrible civil war. In 1919, in the aftermath of the war and the revolution in Russia, the international Marxist movement split into two camps: Communists, who followed the proposals of Lenin for forming parties of the new type, and Socialists, who continued to follow the electoral model of the prewar Social Democratic parties. In Russia itself, the Communist Party, organized according to the Leninist principles of democratic centralism, became the ruling party of the land, justifying its role as necessary to preserve and develop the socialist revolution in Russia. It was this Russian version of communism as a dictatorship of the Communist Party that came to serve as a model for Communist regimes in other parts of the world as well, a model that combined the Marxist idea of central planning with the decidedly un-Marxist idea of a dictatorship by a ruling elite. With the collapse of Communism in the Soviet Union and Eastern Europe, this model has been discredited and with it, rightly or wrongly, much of the appeal of the whole socialist tradition.

# ─── Chapter 5 ───

# The New Liberalism and the Foundations of the Welfare State

At the heart of classical liberalism was the conviction that liberty was conducive to the well-being of humankind. In *The Wealth of Nations* Adam Smith provided powerful arguments for the view that economic liberty was conducive to the greatest possible increase in wealth, and in *On Liberty* John Stuart Mill provided powerful arguments for the view that political and social institutions granting the maximal amount of liberty to individual citizens were likewise conducive to the greatest happiness possible for society as a whole. This conviction about the benefits of liberty became the central battering ram with which the Liberal Party in Britain pushed through the Reform Act of 1832 and the restructuring of British political life consequent upon that act. Nevertheless, by the closing decades of the nineteenth century this same Liberal Party had become the champion for a serious of measures aimed at restricting the liberties of individuals and increasing the powers of the state: laws compelling the education of children, regulating the employment of women and children, compelling adherence to regulations regarding the health and safety of workers, regulating emigration, controlling pollution, and providing for the care of the poor. In "From Freedom to Bondage," an essay published in 1891, Herbert Spencer, a staunch defender of classical liberalism, forcefully charged the British Liberal Party with betrayal of its most fundamental principles.[1]

In fairness to the British Liberals, it should be pointed out that these various measures were widely viewed as necessary responses to the manifest evils of modern industrial life. In the words of one historian of the period, "The social problems consequent upon industrialization were the origin of that administrative state which few anticipated or at heart wished for."[2] Ideologically committed to the idea of laissez-faire, the British Liberals were nonetheless realistic enough to take some steps to address the social problems surrounding them. Nor were British Liberals alone in their retreat from the principle of laissez-faire. In Germany the economist Adolph Wagner pointed to the English experience as a powerful antidote to the ideology of laissez-faire:

> Never has the theory of a laissez-faire state policy and mere self-help for the workers been a more disgraceful fiasco. On that point I should like to refer you to works like those of Marx. Even if you subtract a great deal from the gloomy picture, there still remains enough to make anyone shudder. After such experiences it is incomprehensible to me how a sensible and honorable man can still believe in the sole saving grace of the dogma of laissez-faire. A beautiful "economic harmony" indeed.[3]

The retreat from laissez-faire and the attendant growth of the regulative powers of the state were largely undertaken as a matter of practical necessity. However sweet the laissez-faire society may have appeared in theory, in practice it fell markedly short of the theoretical ideal. In Britain, Germany, the United States, and wherever the system of industrial capitalism had taken root, politicians were forced, as a practical matter, to take some steps to correct the worst evils of the system. Yet the various corrective measures taken were all problematic from the point of view of political philosophy, for all of them, in one way or another, seemed to involve some violation of liberty, and for that reason all of them seemed to conflict with the ideology of classical liberalism. In this chapter we will examine some of the ways political philosophers tried to justify the restraints on liberty implicit in the corrective measures taken by practicing politicians. These various justifications provided the ideological foundations for the modern welfare state.

### Christianity and the Social Gospel

In denouncing laissez-faire economics, Adolph Wagner spoke both as an economist and as a Christian. As an economist, he agreed with Karl Marx and other socialists, who held that free markets based on private ownership tended to amplify differences between rich and poor and largely to condemn the poor to lives of overwork and poverty. As a Christian, Wagner found this outcome to be morally unacceptable. Some Christians took these lessons to heart and became champions of socialism, but Wagner, with his training in economics, was both persuaded of the productive power of free markets and skeptical of the ill-defined solutions offered by the socialists. Consequently, Wagner argued for a middle way between laissez-faire capitalism and socialism, one that preserved private ownership and considerable economic freedom but that also realized fundamental Christian values through the protection of the poor by a system of trade unions, social insurance, and regulated labor markets. A similar middle way between laissez-faire and socialism was championed by Pope Leo XIII in his encyclical *Rerum Novarum* of 1891, which appealed to Christian values of charity and respect for all human beings as requiring measures by society to protect the poor who were without ways of shielding themselves from the vicissitudes of modern life. In the United States a similar position was championed by preachers of the social gospel such as Walter Rauschenbusch, who published his *Christianity and the Social Crisis* in 1907.

As we saw in the previous chapter, conservatives had themselves appealed to Christian values in their critique of classical liberalism. In Britain, much of the early legislation aimed at protecting the poor against the excesses of industrial capitalism had been passed with the support of members of Parliament who belonged to the Conservative Party. But where Conservatives looked for a return to preindustrial forms of life, Christian reformers such as Wagner, Pope Leo, and the American champions of the social gospel saw themselves as leading humankind into new forms of social and political life, forms of life that presupposed the development of modern industry and an extensive nation-state but which nonetheless remained bound by the eternal Christian values of love and charity for all human beings. While Christians certainly do not have a monopoly on these values, the appeal to them as Christian values resonated deeply in the Christian West and provided a socially powerful justification for the emerging welfare state.

## Kantian Ethics

A second source of ideological support for the welfare state comes from the ethics of the late eighteenth-century philosopher Immanuel

Kant. Late nineteenth-century neo-Kantian social reformers found in some of his ideas principles that could be used to justify the kinds of reforms associated with the welfare state.

Kant was himself sharply critical of the utilitarian current within classical liberalism. Kant rejected the utilitarian doctrine that the optimal balance of pleasure over pain was the ultimate moral goal for human beings, regarding the pursuit of pleasure as a goal we share with other animals and as a goal that, in human beings, was superseded by higher moral principles. Like the earlier natural-rights theorists, Kant held that human beings had a capacity for autonomous self-direction. In his view this human capacity for autonomy was bound up with a human capacity to be guided by reason. By the use of reason, human beings are capable of discerning moral laws; as autonomous beings not controlled by internal or external forces, we are capable of either obeying or disobeying those moral laws. Kant thought that this capacity to know and act upon moral rules distinguished human beings from other animals and gave human beings a moral status superior to the status held by other animals and other objects. Where other objects and other animals were properly there for our use, as means to our ends, other human beings existed as ends in themselves. Because of their status as beings capable of discerning and acting upon the moral law, human beings possessed a kind of dignity not held by other animals or objects. They must always be treated with respect and must never be treated as mere means to our ends. Reason shows you, Kant held, that you must "act so that you treat humanity, whether in your own person or in that of another, always as an end and never as a means only."4 Kant argued that this principle gives us another reason for rejecting utilitarianism. Not only do utilitarians err in making pleasure the ultimate goal of morality, they also err in treating human beings as mere means to this end. For the utilitarian, all actions are to be judged in terms of how effective they are at maximizing the total amount of happiness in the world. But if this is so, how we ought to treat ourselves and other human beings is ultimately determined by how such treatment functions as a means to the end of maximizing happiness. On Kant's view, utilitarianism fails grievously as a moral theory because it requires us to view ourselves and other human beings as mere means to the end of maximal happiness.

For similar reasons, a number of late nineteenth- and early twentieth-century philosophers argued that laissez-faire capitalism is morally unacceptable. Within such a system, human labor appears as one commodity among others. Like all commodities, the price of labor is determined by the market forces of supply and demand. And like all commodities utilized in the production of goods and services, labor will be purchased by the capitalist only if the capitalist has an expectation of ultimately making a profit by doing so. As a social system, laissez-faire capitalism institutionalizes the practice of treating human beings—working men, women, and children—as means to the end of making a profit. Such a system seems to flagrantly violate the Kantian maxim that we should never treat human beings as mere means; accordingly, a number of thinkers influenced by Kantian ethics became critics of classical liberalism. Some of these critics embraced versions of socialism, while others, such as Wagner and many of the "new liberals" we will consider below, embraced reforms of capitalism designed to respect the human dignity of labor, including collective bargaining and systems of social insurance typical of the modern welfare state.[5]

**The New Liberalism**

Writing in 1881, the English philosopher T.H. Green offered a defense of the new liberalism embraced by the Liberal Party in Britain in the closing decades of the nineteenth century. Green began his essay by focusing on an apparent contradiction between certain measures supported by the Liberals and the traditional principles of classical liberalism. He pointed to "our Factory Acts, Education Acts, and laws relating to public health" and acknowledged that "they all, in one direction or another, limit a man's power of doing what he will with what he considers his own." Green also acknowledged that "in this respect there is a noticeable difference between the present position of political reformers and that in which they stood a generation ago. Then they fought the fight of reform in the name of individual freedom against class privilege. Their opponents could not with any plausibility invoke the same name against them. Now, in appearance—though, as I shall try to show, not in reality—the case is changed."[6] To liberals weaned on the teachings of Adam Smith and John Stuart Mill, convinced of the benefits of individual freedom, there was something unsettling about the new legislation, which clearly did impose restrictions on individual liberty. As we have already seen, men such as Herbert Spencer, who remained committed to maximizing individual liberty, saw the new liberalism as a betrayal of the core principles of liberalism. Green's essay was an attempt to reply to these fellow liberals. His aim was to show them that the change in principles was only apparent and that in reality the new philosophy remained committed to the core principles of classical liberalism. Green's work was of seminal importance. He influenced a generation of political philosophers in the English-speaking world, including such figures as L.T. Hobhouse in England and John Dewey in the United States. Green also brought together a number of ideas that would become standard parts of liberal political thought. While the reform measures that laid the foundations for the welfare state were largely the work of practical politicians responding to the pressure of the problems of industrial capitalism, it was T.H. Green who provided a philosophical justification of these measures. In the words of H.J. Laski, "It is not true to say that Green gave a new content to liberalism; events themselves had of necessity done that. But it is, I think, true to say that he gave to the idea of positive liberalism its letters of credit."[7] Green's strategy for justifying the regulatory measures favored by the new liberalism turned on the argument that the new measures served the very end of maximizing individual liberty cherished by classical liberalism. One of the key ideas involved in Green's argument was a distinction between negative freedom and positive freedom.

### Negative Freedom and Positive Freedom

Classical liberalism understood freedom as the absence of governmental or social restraints on the actions of individual citizens. Free trade was understood as the absence of restraint on economic activities; freedom of speech was understood as the absence of censorship laws; freedom of religion was understood as the absence of laws prohibiting or requiring certain religious practices. Freedom understood in this way was "negative" freedom in that it indicated the absence of restraints, the absence of coercive legal or social sanctions against the performance of actions by individual citizens. It is this negative freedom that John Stuart Mill had in mind in formulating his harm principle as the principle that should govern all dealings of government and society with the individual. The harm principle says that "the sole end for which mankind are warranted, individually or collectively, in interfering with the liberty of action of any of their number, is self protection."[8] The harm principle is fundamentally a principle of noninterference. It asserts a presumption in favor of the absence of restraints on individual action unless the action in question imposes or threatens to impose harm on some other person. Laws against killing or stealing are morally permissible because actions of these kinds involve harming other people. In such cases society may attempt to restrain the action of the individual by coercion or by coercive threats of punishment, but only where such harms to others are involved is such restraint permitted. The presumption is in favor of freedom, in favor of the absence of restraint.

Green did not deny the importance of negative freedom. However, he did not think the understanding of freedom as the absence of humanly imposed restraints was an adequate understanding of the true nature of freedom. In his essay "Liberal Legislation and Freedom of Contract," written in 1881, Green offered this analysis of the true nature of freedom:

> We shall probably all agree that freedom, rightly understood, is the greatest of blessings—that its attainment is the true end of all our effort as citizens. But when we thus speak of freedom, we should consider carefully what we mean by it. We do not mean merely freedom from restraint or compulsion. We do not mean merely freedom to do as we like irrespectively of what it is that we like. We do not mean a freedom that can be enjoyed by one man or one set of men at the cost of a loss of freedom to others. When we speak of freedom as something to be so highly prized, we mean a positive power or capacity of doing or enjoying something worth doing or enjoying, and that, too, something that we do or enjoy in common with others.[9]

This is a very complex statement, one that draws upon the work of the German philosopher G.W.F. Hegel. While any attempt to fairly explicate the philosophy of Hegel in any detail would take us far beyond the bounds of this study (and perhaps beyond the bounds of what is humanly possible), in what follows we will nonetheless attempt to come to a workable understanding of what Green has in mind by the idea of freedom as a "positive power or capacity," drawing on some of the ideas of Hegel insofar as this is necessary.

At the heart of the idea of positive freedom is the idea that freedom involves some kind of self-expression or self-realization. A free action is one that has its origins in the self. The self feels the action to be free because it springs from within and is not imposed by some external force. Human beings are by nature active beings who delight in expressing themselves through action in the world. The child expresses itself in its actions and finds joy in the development of its capacities and the realization of these capacities in action. The adult finds satisfaction in labor or creative activity that expresses talents and abilities. To be human is to have a need for self-expression, to find joy in self-expression, and to feel free in action that achieves self-expression.

This idea of freedom as self-expression is a core part of what Green, following Hegel, has in mind by the idea of positive freedom. But it is not all that is involved. Not all actions that spring from inner causes are free actions. The drug addict has a powerful craving that comes from within, but action based on that craving is likely not to be experienced by the addict as free action. Indeed, the addict may experience the inner urge as a kind of compulsion that robs him of his freedom. In somewhat the same way, the ordinary person, in response to intense fear welling up from inside during a time of danger, may run away from responsibilities and subsequently feel ashamed of this. But in this case the action of running away would not be experienced as free action. The craving of the drug addict and the fear of the person in danger are apt to be experienced as alien forces not belonging to the true self. Freedom, then, seems to consist in action in the world that expresses or realizes the self in a way that the self would affirm as an expression of itself.

But what is the true self? The utilitarians tend to think of the self as a given. It is conceived as a thing that finds itself in the world with a given bundle of wants and desires, the satisfaction of which will give it pleasure. Hegel and Green reject this view of the self as a pleasure-seeking social atom. On their view, human beings have ideals and aims that cannot be reduced to the maximizing of pleasure. Further, they conceive of these human beings as socially constructed selves. We are born into families, nationalities, religions, races, genders, and social classes. The way we look at the world and the way we feel about it are products of our historical circumstances. In a sense, each of us is an expression of our time. We feel and understand ourselves to be a part of a people with a past, with traditions, sacred responsibilities to one another, and historically situated aims and ideals. The daughter of a human-rights activist imprisoned by a cruel dictator vows to herself to struggle for democracy for herself and for her children and for her children's children. To be sure, gaining democracy gives her pleasure, but it is not for this feeling of pleasure that she struggles for democracy. In the view of Hegel and Green, the true self is that part of each of us that strives to realize in the world aspirations that reflect "something worth doing or enjoying" in the specific social and historical circumstances in which we find ourselves. We are truly free to the extent that we succeed in acting on impulses from within us that have such aims.

Green was a democrat. He believed that ordinary people had within them talents and abilities worthy of finding expression in their lives. But without the resources necessary to develop those talents, or without the opportunities to express them, people are not truly free. The person with athletic ability who never has access to the resources necessary to develop that ability is no less unfree than the person who is barred from athletic competition by governmental decree. Negative freedom is important for Green, but it is important as a means to an end: the end of self-expression or self-realization. Positive freedom is not the negation but the complement of negative freedom. Positive freedom involves provision to the individual of those resources and opportunities necessary for the development and expression of his or her talents and abilities. Thus, in defending the compulsory elementary education mandated by the Education Acts, Green held that a person cannot be held to be free to develop his faculties without "a command of certain elementary arts and knowledge."[10] Though compulsory education does limit the freedom of parents to contract their children out to labor in the mills, and though the taxation needed to fund compulsory education does limit the freedom of taxpayers to do what they will with what they own, still, in Green's view, the real result of compulsory education is an increase, not a decrease, in freedom. Children who lacked an elementary education would be as effectively barred from life's opportunities as if they were prohibited from those opportunities by law. In this way, Green argued, the legislation supported by the new liberals remains true to the love of liberty at the core of classical liberalism. The new liberalism was not a betrayal of liberalism but a fulfillment of it.

Green's ideas were widely influential. In Britain, L.T. Hobhouse contrasted the merely negative freedom embodied in freedom of contract with the "effective freedom" championed by the new liberalism, and he supported his thinking with an "organic" theory of the self based in part on the ideas of Green and Hegel.[11] In the United States, the early John Dewey "echoed the conviction of Green and other idealists [British Hegelians] that, properly conceived, freedom was the opportunity to make the best of oneself as a social being."[12] But while it is historically true that Hegelian ideas provided at least part of the underpinning for the new liberalism of Green, Hobhouse, and Dewey, it is possible to argue for the principles of new liberalism without recourse to heavy doses of Hegelian ideas. In his introduction to T.H. Green's *Principles of Political Obligation*, A.D. Lindsay observed that "Green and his fellow-idealists represent the renewed liberalism of the last quarter of the nineteenth century. They are all of them, for all their Platonism and Hegelianism, in the succession of the Utilitarians. They were all fundamentally individualists and democrats."[13] There is a good deal of truth in what Lindsay says here. In the section that follows we will see how the principles of classical liberalism can be extended to encompass the new liberalism without recourse to Hegelian philosophy.

**Utility and Liberty**

Within classical liberalism, the utilitarian current came to dominate over the earlier natural-rights tradition. From the utilitarian perspective of Adam Smith and John Stuart Mill, liberty was valuable because it was conducive to happiness. In this perspective, liberty is valuable as a means to an end. The utilitarians themselves conceived of this end hedonistically as the maximization of human happiness. Following Hegel, Green and others of the new liberals were critical of this hedonistic framework, viewing it as too narrow to capture the rich diversity of ends toward which human beings aspired. From their point of view, human beings aimed at ends such as artistic expression, beauty, knowledge, and justice, which were not reducible to "pleasure" or "happiness." In place of the hedonistic end postulated by utilitarianism, the new liberals conceived of the end toward which political institutions should be striving as something like the socially maximal development of the talents and abilities of all human beings. To paraphrase the words of Marx, who, like the new liberals, built on Hegelian foundations, the end sought was one in which the free development of each individual was realized as much as possible.[14]

Now, this end, the socially maximal development of the talents and abilities of all human beings, is not far from the goal of "happiness," at least as it was understood by the classical liberalism of John Stuart

Mill. Mill distinguished between higher and lower pleasures, ranking those pleasures humans shared with other animals as less desirable than those pleasures of the mind and spirit that were uniquely human.[15] In his view, it was a fact about human nature that humans were happier to the extent that they were able to cultivate and act upon their higher faculties. Given this view of human nature, a society providing for the maximal development of the talents and abilities of all of its members would be a society maximizing happiness.

It is also important to remember that the justification for individual liberty offered by Mill is one that makes liberty a means to the realization of the end of maximizing happiness. Because the new liberals shared Mill's view of human nature, and because, like Mill, they shared the view that individual liberty was valuable as a means to the achievement of the social good, they could agree with classical liberalism in arguing for a large arena for individual liberty.

There was also an important structural similarity between classical and new liberalism with respect to the justification of individual freedom. Like the classical liberalism of Mill and the utilitarians, the new liberalism worked within a consequentialist framework. Both judged the value of political institutions by their consequences. For both, freedom was justified as a means to an end. This being so, freedom was justified only insofar as it truly contributed to the social good. While it is true that the new liberalism did impose some restrictions on the absolute liberty of individuals to contract with one another, Green could answer those critics of the new liberalism who saw it as a betrayal of classical liberalism with the claim that the new liberalism remained true to the goal of classical liberalism, the achieving of "the social good against class interests."[16] While it is true that Green and other philosophers who tried to justify the measures supported by the new liberals appealed to the ideas of Hegel, a straightforward consequentialist argument was embedded within their reasoning that did not rely heavily on Hegel.

## Coercion Masked as Liberty

In a passage in *The Wealth of Nations,* Adam Smith discusses disputes between employers (masters) and their workmen.

> In all such disputes the masters can hold out much longer. A landlord, a farmer, a master manufacturer, a merchant, though they did not employ

a single workman, could generally live a year or two upon the stocks which they have already acquired. Many workmen could not subsist a week, few could subsist a month, and scarce any a year without employment. In the long-run the workman may be as necessary to his master as his master is to him; but the necessity is not so immediate.[17]

This inequality in the bargaining position of employer and employee also played a role in the philosophical justification of the reform measures supported by the new liberals. Concerning the bargain between the capitalist and the workers, L.T. Hobhouse said, "The bargain is a forced bargain. The weaker man consents as one slipping over a precipice might consent to give all his fortune to one who will throw him a rope on no other terms."[18] Coerced by the necessity of feeding and housing himself and his family, the worker must accept the terms offered by the capitalist. Though the contract is voluntary in the sense that it is up to the worker whether or not he agrees to it, the voluntary nature of the contract masks an underlying unfreedom. In concerning themselves only with the absence of governmental coercion, classical liberals turned a blind eye to this masked coercion of circumstance. New liberals argued that a consistent liberalism, one that was truly committed to the value of liberty, would recognize the necessity of limiting the coercive power of circumstances in order to make freedom real for the masses of working men and women.

These various currents—Christian charity, Kantian morality, the idea of real freedom as positive freedom, and a greater sensitivity to the coercion of circumstance—all provided the new liberals with justifications for the emerging powers of the welfare state. For thinkers rooted in the liberal tradition, it was the understanding of real freedom as positive freedom that was decisive. Less central to the liberal tradition but more popular with the poor and the working classes was the conviction that the measures adopted by the new liberalism were requirements of elementary justice. In the next chapter we will survey some basic ideas about what justice is.

# — Chapter 6 —

# Justice

How should wealth be distributed among the members of a society? This is a question of distributive justice. It is not a question that was central to either the natural-rights tradition or the utilitarian tradition. For classical liberalism, founded on these two traditions, liberty and the pursuit of happiness were the fundamental ends of political life. The new liberalism proclaimed its adherence to these same liberal values, but, appearing as it did at the end of the nineteenth century, when the manifest contrast between rich and poor had provoked anarchist and socialist demands for a revolutionary redistribution of wealth, it could not avoid the issue of distributive justice. Reflecting on the existence of poverty in the midst of plenty, the new liberal L.T. Hobhouse held that the prevention of avoidable suffering was an end all members of society were obligated to pursue.[1]

The progressive income tax was one of the means by which the new liberals hoped to advance this end. The progressive income tax, which taxes higher incomes at higher rates than lower incomes, aimed at reducing the gap between rich and poor by putting the greater part of the burden of financing government on those with higher incomes. In 1848, when it appeared as one of the measures recommended by Marx and Engels in *The Manifesto of the Communist Party,* the progressive income tax was a radical idea. By the first decade of the twentieth century, the principle of progressive taxation had become a common feature in the new liberalism that dominated the thinking of the times. In 1909 the progressive income tax was introduced in Britain, and in 1913, by constitutional amendment, it was introduced in the United States.

The case for the progressive income tax was simple enough. It rested upon the conviction that the existing inequalities of wealth were morally unacceptable. By taxing the rich more heavily than the poor, the progressive income tax reduced somewhat the inequalities in spendable income resulting from private property and free markets. In the 1930s governments in many of the developed capitalist countries introduced public subsidies for food, housing, child care, education, health care, and unemployment insurance in an attempt to deal with the widespread misery caused by the great depression. Funded by progressive income taxes, these measures were defended as a means for redistributing income from the rich to the poor.[2] But how far should this redistribution go? What would be a just distribution of wealth?

**Utilitarian Considerations**

The principle of utility tells us that we ought to do whatever will maximize the total amount of happiness. Insofar as the principle of utility focuses on maximizing the total amount of happiness produced, utilitarianism is, in a sense, fundamentally oblivious to how this happiness is distributed among the various members of society. For the utilitarian, a just distribution of wealth would be that distribution that maximizes the total amount of happiness. If it were to turn out that awarding all wealth to some single individual produced more total happiness than any other possible distribution of wealth, then, for the utilitarian, that assignment of all wealth to that single individual would be morally optimal and therefore just. But, of course, it is extremely unlikely that a system that awarded all wealth to some particular individual would actually maximize total happiness. The science of economics provides a good reason for thinking that such a radically unequal distribution of wealth would not maximize happiness and would not therefore, on utilitarian grounds, be morally optimal or just.

The principle of economics that is relevant here is the principle of diminishing marginal utility. For a hungry person a bowl of soup produces a good deal of happiness, or utility. A second bowl of soup, though still welcome, will produce a little less happiness than the first, and subsequent bowls of soup will produce even less happiness. In general, the more of a thing one consumes, the less happiness will be produced by each additional unit of the thing consumed. Now, suppose we consider the redistribution of wealth from the rich to the poor with this principle of diminishing marginal utility in mind. Suppose we take

$100 from some millionaire and give it to an impoverished student who has not had a decent meal in weeks. The student, who has no money, will gain considerable happiness from the $100. To be sure, the millionaire from whom the $100 is taken will experience some unhappiness over the loss of this quantity of money, but because the millionaire has so much money left over, the unhappiness will not be great. For the student, the $100 is like the first bowl of soup for the hungry person. For the millionaire, the loss of the $100 is like the loss of the tenth bowl of soup for a satiated person. In short, by taking from the millionaire and giving to the student, we produce a greater amount of happiness than would have been produced without this redistribution of wealth. In general, then, it would seem that the principle of utility, combined with the principle of diminishing marginal utility, provides a strong case for taking from the rich and giving to the poor. But how far, according to utilitarianism, should this redistribution go?

At first glance it might appear that the utilitarian would be led by the principle of diminishing marginal utility to advocate an egalitarian distribution of wealth, one that assigned an equal amount of wealth to every individual. After all, so long as any inequalities exist, were we to take from the individual who has more and give to the individual who has less, the principle of diminishing marginal utility suggests that total happiness would be increased. However, there are at least two reasons why this might not be so.

One of these reasons arises out of a problem known as the problem of interpersonal comparisons of utility. To decide whether or not a transfer of wealth from individual A to individual B increases total happiness, we must somehow measure the happiness lost by A and that gained by B. But how could we do that? The principle of diminishing marginal utility gives us a reason to think that for each individual, A and B, the amount of happiness produced for that individual diminishes with each additional unit of a particular good consumed by that individual. But it might be that the tenth unit of good X produces more happiness in individual A than the first unit of good X produces in individual B. The principle of diminishing marginal utility allows us to compare units of happiness produced by additional units of a good only within a particular individual. It provides no basis for comparing the amount of happiness produced in one individual by a unit of good X with the amount of happiness produced in another individual by a unit of good X no matter how many units of good X either individual initially possessed. It might be, for example, that individual A is a miser who loves money very, very much, while individual B is a carefree soul who is largely indifferent to wealth. If this is so, then even though the principle of diminishing marginal utility is true, it might nonetheless be that a transfer of wealth from the wealthy but miserly A to the poor but carefree B would actually cause a net loss in the total amount of happiness produced. Since we have no way of knowing whether or not a proposed redistribution of wealth would increase total happiness, some have concluded that the utilitarian argument for an egalitarian distribution discussed above fails. Others, while acknowledging the theoretical difficulty, have argued that for practical purposes we may assume that human beings are more or less alike and that equal amounts of happiness or unhappiness would be produced in each by similar circumstances.

Still, the utilitarian argument for redistribution faces a second difficulty, one that seems to provide a powerful argument against an egalitarian distribution of wealth. This second difficulty concerns the problem of incentives. Suppose we were to adopt a policy of redistributing wealth from the rich to the poor until everyone had an equal share of the total wealth produced by society as a whole. Such a policy is likely to undermine incentives to work. Why should you work to produce wealth if what you produce is going to be taken from you by the policy of redistribution? Why not just lie around doing nothing, since you will receive from the policy of redistribution just as much as the most productive member of society receives? The radically egalitarian policy of redistribution leaves individuals with no incentive to work, and, because this is so, the egalitarian policy is likely to result in a sharp reduction in the total amount of wealth produced and in a corresponding reduction in the total amount of happiness produced. For this reason the utilitarian who aims at maximizing total happiness is not likely to champion an egalitarian distribution of wealth, no matter how attractive that solution may initially have appeared.

What, then, would be a just distribution of wealth on utilitarian principles? Setting aside the problem of interpersonal comparisons, a plausible answer might emerge if we combine recognition of the positive effect on total happiness resulting from redistribution, based on the principle of diminishing marginal utility, with recognition of the positive effect on total happiness of a system of incentives that rewards productive activity.

Imagine some distribution of wealth and income resulting from the operation of a free-market system. Such a system provides individuals with incentives to engage in productive activity. Now suppose we impose a modest progressive income tax on this system, using the taxes raised to subsidize food, housing, education, and medical care for those with the lowest incomes. What will be the effect of this progressive income tax on total happiness? We now know there will be at least two effects. On one hand, the tax will to some extent reduce incentives to engage in productive activity and accordingly reduce somewhat the total amount of wealth produced and thereby also reduce somewhat the total amount of happiness. At the same time, by the reasoning from the principle of diminishing marginal utility, there will be to some extent an increase in happiness resulting from the shift of income from the rich to the poor. Assuming that we have some way of comparing the reduction in happiness caused by weakened incentives with the increase in happiness caused by redistribution, the utilitarian can determine whether or not the tax produced a net gain or loss in total happiness. If the reduction exceeds the gain, then the tax rates should be reduced. If the gain exceeds the reduction, then the tax rates should be increased. In this way, by a series of adjustments, the utilitarian could arrive at a solution to the problem of justice in the distribution of wealth. The just solution would be the tax rate that maximized total happiness.

There are, of course, enormous difficulties in ascertaining just what rate of taxation might in fact maximize total happiness, including how to make interpersonal comparisons of utility and how to measure the effects of taxation on incentives to engage in productive activity. Nevertheless, by considerations of the kind sketched above, utilitarianism may be able to provide at least a theoretical answer to the question of how wealth should be distributed in a just society. Still, many philosophers are not prepared to accept the utilitarian theory as an adequate account of justice. In the next section we will consider some of the reasons that have led these philosophers to think that the utilitarian theory fails.

## Nonutilitarian Conceptions of Justice

Imagine a society consisting of two people. Suppose they are equally capable of performing productive work and equally endowed with natural resources and the tools necessary to make use of those resources.

Suppose one individual works hard and produces enough to make possible a secure and comfortable existence. Suppose the other individual passes his days lying in a hammock. Now, how should the total wealth produced be divided between these individuals? The utilitarian solution would seem to say that we should take some from the productive individual and give it to the unproductive idler. But is this really just? Doesn't the individual who worked to produce the wealth deserve to keep it? Isn't it an injustice to take from this individual a portion of what that person deserves, even if giving that portion over to the unproductive idler does increase the total amount of happiness? Considerations of this kind have led many philosophers to think that the utilitarian account of justice is radically defective.

### Kant's Critique of Utilitarianism

As we have already seen, the great eighteenth-century German philosopher Immanuel Kant was a firm critic of utilitarianism. For utilitarianism, what has intrinsic value is happiness: the optimal balance of pleasure over pain. All other things have only extrinsic value: value as a means of maximizing happiness. The principle of utility requires us to maximize the total amount of happiness produced. Now imagine that a surgeon has five patients. Two are in desperate need of kidneys; two are in desperate need of lungs, and the fifth is in desperate need of a heart transplant. Suppose that the surgeon comes upon an individual, Isaac, who happens to have kidneys, lungs, and a heart that would be perfect matches for the five patients in desperate need. Suppose further that Isaac has no particular talents to offer humankind, and no friends or family who would miss him. If the surgeon were a utilitarian, he might think that he ought to kill Isaac and save the lives of the five patients. After all, wouldn't this maximize happiness? To be sure, there are a host of complicating considerations here, involving the illegality of killing, the risks to the surgeon of being detected, and so forth. But in Kant's view, what is wrong with utilitarianism is that it even tempts us to consider sacrificing one person for the good of the whole. In contrast, as we have already seen, Kant advances a principle that we should always treat human beings "never simply as a means, but always at the same time as an end."[3] Kant thought of human beings as having intrinsic worth, and because of this he thought that there were certain things that it is wrong to do to a human being even if so doing would increase the total amount of happiness in the world. For the surgeon to use our hypothetical Isaac as a source for organs for the good of others would be to treat Isaac as a mere means, to fail to give him the respect and the rights to which he is entitled by his position as an end in himself.

Kant also thought that utilitarianism was radically wrong in its theory of retributive justice. Retributive justice includes issues pertaining to what is just in the punishment of wrongdoers. For the utilitarian, what justifies punishing the wrongdoer is that this provides him and others with incentives for refraining from wrongdoing in the future, and thus promotes the happiness of society as a whole. In Kant's view, this way of looking at things ignores what is really the whole foundation of retributive justice. For Kant, what counts is not the effect of the punishment in promoting the happiness of society but what the wrongdoer deserves. Kant thought that we human beings were capable of freely choosing between right and wrong. When we choose to do what is wrong, we deserve punishment—not because this will deter crime in the future (though indeed punishment may have that effect) but because we deserve the punishment based upon what we did in the past.

Here with the idea of "deserving something" we have a concept that links retributive justice with our earlier discussion of distributive justice and both of these with Kant's idea of human beings as ends in themselves. In Kant's view, human beings are not like other parts of the natural world. We have in us a capacity to know right from wrong and to freely choose between them. It is this capacity that gives us a higher importance than mere things or animals, which have no such capacity. Our existence has a moral dimension to it that is lacking in the existence of mere things or animals. It is because of this that we must be treated with respect as ends in ourselves, and it is because of this capacity that we can deserve punishment or reward for the actions we have performed. The person who works hard *deserves* the wealth she has produced. The criminal who freely chooses to do what he knows is wrong *deserves* punishment. In each case, what is deserved is based upon what was done in the past. Justice, which is giving to each what he deserves, is backward-looking. Unlike the principle of utility, which aims at maximizing happiness in the future and so considers only the probable future consequences of our actions, the principle of justice looks to the past. It considers not the future consequences of punishment or reward, but rather the kind of action that was done in the past and the punishment or reward that is deserved by actions of that kind.[4]

### Alternative Principles of Distributive Justice

Our very brief consideration of Kant's views is meant to raise the possibility that justice is something fundamentally different from the maximization of happiness. Very roughly put, justice is getting what you deserve. But, then, what is it that you deserve? Let us briefly consider some possible principles of justice, each reflecting different views about what is deserved.

### Egalitarianism

We have already given some consideration to the egalitarian solution to the problem of distribution. It recommends itself as the "obvious" solution for distributing benefits and burdens in many social situations. How should pieces of cake be distributed among the guests? What portion of the fare should each of the passengers who share a cab from the airport pay? If we agree with Kant that human beings are ends in themselves, deserving of respect and common fundamental rights on the basis of this shared humanity, we might think that, in virtue of this common moral status, each person deserves equal treatment. But there are serious objections to egalitarianism as a principle to govern the distribution of wealth produced in a society. As we have already seen, the egalitarian principle seems to undermine incentives and seems to violate justice in taking from those who contribute to society and giving to those who do not.

### To Each According to Contribution

In light of the difficulties of egalitarianism, it might be thought that justice consists in rewarding each in proportion to the contribution made by each. We might still acknowledge the truth of the Kantian view that all humans are equally ends in themselves by pointing out that the principle of contribution does treat everyone equally in a sense—equally rewarding equal contribution. One of the most prominent supporters of the principle of contribution is, surprisingly, Karl Marx. Though Marx is often pictured as an egalitarian, in the *Critique of the Gotha Program,* which contains his most explicit comments on distribution in post-capitalist societies, Marx endorses two distinct principles, neither of which is egalitarian. Marx holds that the principle of contribution is the principle of justice appropriate to govern distribution in the immediate post-capitalist society. "The individual producer receives back from society . . . exactly what he gives to it."[5] In Marx's view this is an advance over the distribution of wealth under capitalism, since capitalism handsomely rewards the owner of substantial means of production who spends his life lounging on the Riviera. Still, there are problems with the principle of contribution. After all, some people are physically or mentally more gifted than others. For them, contributing a given amount to society requires little effort, while for a less gifted fellow citizen contributing the same amount requires an effort of heroic proportions. Is it fair to reward these two individuals equally? Does the person who makes the heroic effort not deserve more than the person who contributes the same with little effort?

*To Each According to Effort*

Perhaps, then, the truly just principle of distribution would reward each individual in proportion to the effort that individual expended in making a contribution to the social good. After all, it is this effort that lies within the power of the kind of freedom postulated by Kant. I cannot choose my innate mental or physical talents. Nor can I, by my free choice, guarantee the successful acquisition of a mental or physical skill. All I can do is make the effort to use the innate talents that I have and the effort to acquire those skills that I lack. Insofar as what I deserve is based on my free will, and only my effort lies within the control of that free will, it seems reasonable to make effort rather than contribution the basis for my share of the social wealth. But even here there are difficulties. Suppose two individuals make the same effort to contribute to the social good, but that one of those individuals, through no fault of her own, suffers from a serious medical condition requiring expensive treatment. To reward the two individuals equally on the basis of their equal effort ignores the different needs facing the two. If one must spend nearly all of her income on medical care, is it just that she be reduced to poverty while the other lives a life of comfort?

*From Each According to Ability, to Each According to Needs*

In his discussion of distribution in postcapitalist societies, Marx recognizes the difficulty that is becoming evident in our own brief survey of alternative principles of distribution. Justice demands that we treat like cases alike, but people have many different dimensions. Contribution, effort, and need are three such dimensions. People who are alike in one of these dimensions are apt to be different in another. Marx puts the point this way: "Right by its very nature can consist only in the application of an equal standard; but unequal individuals . . . are measurable only by an equal standard in so far as they are brought under an equal point of view, are taken from one definite side only."[6] For this reason, Marx concludes, any standard of right or justice is doomed to failure. Accordingly—though, as we have seen, he endorsed the contribution principle as the best principle for governing the immediate postcapitalist society—Marx looks forward to a higher phase of communist society in which the principle of distribution governing society will be "from each according to his ability, to each according to his need."[7] This particular principle of distribution recognizes the necessary inadequacy of any single dimensional standard of justice. In a sense it combines two standards: on one hand, it demands equal effort from each individual (I take contribution according to ability as an equal-effort principle), while on the other hand, it rewards individuals on the basis of their needs. But this very separation of the standard for contribution and the standard for distribution tends to weaken the incentives for productive contribution. There are also serious problems about how we might measure effort and need. For these reasons, perhaps, most of the former Communist countries remained under the sway of the principle of contribution, with the former USSR going so far as to institute piece-rate systems according to which the pay a worker receives is directly proportional to the amount she produces.[8]

## Rawls's Theory of Justice

Published in 1971, John Rawls's *A Theory of Justice* is widely regarded as one of the most important works in political philosophy of the twentieth century. By what principles would a just society be organized? Rawls suggests that we approach this question by asking ourselves what kind of rules we would choose to govern our society were we to take part in a sort of founding constitutional convention aimed at reaching an agreement about the fundamental rules for the society in which we would live. Of course, were we really to do such a thing, we would be likely to advocate fundamental rules that would serve our particular situation. Thus, for example, if I happen to suffer from some serious and debilitating illness, I am apt to insist that the fundamental rules must guarantee adequate medical care and income for people who are unable to work. On the other hand, if I am in good health and endowed with a rich array of talents, I might be inclined to insist that our future society should be based on the principle of contribution. In order to remove such biases from our thinking, Rawls asks us to consider what fundamental rules would be agreed upon by individuals who were operating behind a veil of ignorance about the particular aspects of their individual situations in life.

Suppose there was a group of persons engaged in a founding constitutional convention. Suppose also that each of these persons had a great deal of knowledge about what human beings are like, about how different economic and political arrangements would work, and about how different specific abilities and debilities actually affect human beings. However, suppose also that none of these individuals knows what his or her own specific abilities and debilities will be and that none knows the particular position in life he or she will fill. This is what Rawls calls the veil of ignorance. We are to imagine people entering into a social contract, an agreement about the fundamental rules that will govern the society in which they live, behind such a veil of ignorance. Rawls's central idea is that just principles are those that would be chosen by individuals forming a social contract behind such a veil of ignorance. The principles chosen under such conditions would be just because individuals forming a social contract under such conditions would face the possibility of filling any one of the possible social roles existing in the future society. Accordingly, each person entering into the contract would want to be sure that every possible social role was fairly treated.

What rules would be chosen by individuals entering into a social contract behind such a veil of ignorance? Surprisingly enough, Rawls thinks he can show that some fairly specific fundamental rules would be chosen. These rules then constitute the fundamental principles of justice in Rawls's theory. Rawls formulates these fundamental rules in this way:

> First Principle—Each person is to have an equal right to the most extensive total system of equal basic liberties compatible with a similar system of liberty for all.
> Second Principle—Social and economic inequalities are to be arranged so that they are both:

(a) to the greatest benefit of the least advantaged, and
(b) attached to offices and positions open to all under conditions of
fair equality of opportunity.[9]

The basic liberties mentioned in the first principle are civil and political rights, such as freedoms of religion, speech, press, and assembly, the right to vote and run for office, rights of due process in civil and criminal proceedings, and freedom to move from one place to another. These are the core liberties championed by classical liberals and new liberals alike. It should also be noted here that in clauses added just below those quoted above, Rawls explicitly acknowledges the priority of liberty over other social and economic goods. That is, on his theory, it would not be just to sacrifice the basic liberties of anyone in order to attain greater social wealth. Rawls would reject the claims of some Communists that restrictions of liberty are just because they improve the lot of the poor. In acknowledging this "priority of liberty" over social and economic goods, Rawls shows his allegiance to liberalism, which has traditionally made liberty its most sacred value. We shall not pause here to examine Rawls's argument for the priority of liberty since our main concern is with Rawls's second principle, which concerns the issue of justice in the distribution of wealth, the issue with which we have been concerned in this chapter.[10]

Rawls's second principle concerns the arrangement of social and economic inequalities. Clause (b) stipulates that such inequalities are to be attached to offices and positions open to all under conditions of fair equality of opportunity. This too follows a classic principle of liberal thought. It is best understood in terms of what it rejects. In the class-divided societies of late medieval Europe, certain positions, and the income and status that went with them, were reserved for members of the hereditary aristocracy. One of the central demands of the French Revolution was that all these positions should be open to talent—that it was not just to reserve these positions for members of certain families and to exclude all others from competing for them. In a similar vein, most of us would agree that it is not just to exclude people from positions because of their race, as was widely done in South Africa and the United States until quite recent times. Clause (b) is meant to exclude discrimination of this kind.

But clause (b) goes further than this. It demands not just absence of discrimination but also the provision of the minimal resources necessary to give all citizens a fair chance at filling desirable positions. This is what Rawls has in mind in calling for "fair" equality of opportunity. Suppose, for example, that a country removes legal barriers that prevented members of an oppressed group from being considered for some positions. But suppose also that members of the group in question are too poor to pay for the education needed to successfully compete for these positions. In this case the members of the group remain effectively excluded from those positions even if the explicit legal discrimination against them has been removed. Since it is a matter of genetic luck whether one is born into such a poor group or into a group rich in resources, justice requires that we take some steps to make the competition for positions more equal. For this reason, Rawls's principle of "fair equality of opportunity" requires, in addition to nondiscrimination, the provision of the resources necessary to genuinely compete for positions. It should also be noted that Rawls gives satisfaction of clause (b) priority over satisfaction of clause (a), here again reflecting his deep attachment to traditional liberal values.[11]

We are now ready to focus on clause (a) of Rawls's Second Principle of justice. Assume that we have agreed that our top priority is to guarantee basic liberties to all citizens and that we have also agreed that all positions are to be open to fair equality of opportunity. Assuming that these arrangements are in place, clause (a) now says that social and economic inequalities are to be arranged so that they work to the greatest benefit of the least advantaged. Rawls calls this principle the difference principle since it concerns inequalities, or differences, in the distribution of wealth. We can begin to see what this difference principle says by going back to our earlier discussion of the progressive income tax.

Recall the utilitarian argument for a progressive income tax based on the principle of diminishing marginal utility and the aim of maximizing happiness. By taxing the rich and giving subsidies to the poor we lessen the degree of income inequality and increase total happiness. But this works only up to a point. If the tax is too odious, it will undermine incentives to work, resulting in the production of less wealth and consequently reducing the total amount of happiness. From a utilitarian point of view, the best solution is the one that maximizes total happiness, and this maximal point will be reached when the tax rates are set at precisely that point where any further gains from redistribution would be offset by greater losses resulting from the undermining of incentives.

Now suppose that you are engaged behind the veil of ignorance in entering into a fundamental social contract with other individuals. Would you agree to a progressive income tax to be determined along the utilitarian lines sketched above? Rawls claims that a rational person would not agree to this utilitarian solution. Rawls's reasoning is fairly simple to understand. At first glance it might seem that the utilitarian solution is the one that would be chosen. The utilitarian solution maximizes the total amount of income produced. If we assume a stable population, the utilitarian solution also maximizes the average amount of income for individuals in a society organized according to it. Since each person engaged in forming the social contract has no information regarding the probability of his or her occupying any particular position in the actual future society, each position appears as an equally likely possible future for each individual. Since the utilitarian solution regarding the extent of income differences maximizes average income, it would appear that the rational individual would chose the utilitarian solution on the grounds that that solution gives the highest average amount of income over the whole range of equally possible outcomes.

The problem with the utilitarian solution is that while it is true that it maximizes average income, it is also possible that it allows for inequalities in income so great that those at the bottom of the income scale have lives of unacceptably poor quality.

To see how this might be so, consider a society organized under the principle of strict equality of income. We have seen already that this severely undermines incentives to work. Suppose, then, that we permit some inequality in incomes by reducing the tax transfers from market winners to market losers. Suppose that this increases incentives to work, increases total wealth produced, and raises the income levels of everyone. Because the total wealth produced is greater, even though the tax rates on the rich are less, the amount raised by taxes and transferred to the poor is greater than before, and hence even those who now find themselves at the bottom of the income scale are better off than they were before inequalities in income were allowed. Suppose, on the basis of this happy outcome, we reduce the tax rates even further, allowing greater inequalities in income, and suppose this second tax reform has the same effect as the first, making even the poorest individuals better off than they were before. Now suppose we continue reducing the tax rates, thereby increasing incentives and consequently increasing the total amount of wealth produced. Imagine that we continue in this fashion until we reach a point where a reduction in the tax rate has the effect of increasing the total amount produced but decreasing the incomes of the worse-off members of society. Suppose that the reduction in subsidies going to the poor exceeds the share of the increased pretax income going to the poor. In short, we have reached a point where increases in inequality will increase the total income produced but decrease the income going to those persons at the lowest income levels. The utilitarian solution, which aims at maximizing average income, would countenance this latest increase in income inequalities. Rawls's difference principle would not. According to the difference principle, social and economic inequalities are to be arranged so that they are to the greatest benefit of the least advantaged. In our imagined sequence of reductions in the tax rates, the difference principle would approve of the increased inequalities produced by those earlier reductions because they made the poorest individuals better off than they were before the increased inequality was introduced. However, the increased inequalities made by our imagined final reductions in the tax rates made those at the bottom of the income scale worse off than they were before these inequalities were introduced. Hence, these inequalities would be unacceptable to Rawls's difference principle, even though they might actually increase average income for the society as a whole.

Rawls argues that the rational individual entering into a social contract behind the veil of ignorance would prefer the difference principle to the utilitarian maximization of average income. So long as inequalities satisfy the difference principle, even those at the bottom of the income scale are better off for permitting those inequalities. But if we adopt the strategy of maximizing average utility, we risk finding ourselves at the bottom of an income scale based on inequalities that make us worse off than we would have been had those inequalities not been permitted. Rawls thinks that a rational person would not want to risk this possibility and would opt for the difference principle, which guarantees the best worst outcome. That is, adopting the difference principle guarantees that even if the individual has the bad luck to find himself at the bottom of the income scale in the actual society, this bottom will be better than the bottom in any of the other possible social systems. This is because the difference principle allows inequalities only if they make the poorest individuals better off than they otherwise would have been. Rawls argues that a rational person would play it safe, choosing the difference principle over more risky alternatives such as the utilitarian solution.

## Criticisms of Rawls's Theory of Justice

One common criticism of Rawls's theory is that it really provides no satisfactory basis for the claim that a rational person behind the veil of ignorance would choose the difference principle over the utilitarian solution or over other possible positions regarding acceptable levels of inequality. Rawls argues for the difference principle over the utilitarian principle on the grounds that the difference principle is less risky, guaranteeing the best possible worst outcome. But while the utilitarian solution includes the risk of a worse outcome, it also includes a greater chance at a better outcome. Which strategy would a rational individual prefer?

Rawls's claim that the rational individual would prefer the difference principle works only if we think the rational person is strongly averse to risk, but this appears to be more a matter of psychology than rationality. The rational risk-aversive person should choose the difference principle, and the rational risk taker should choose the average utility principle. But if this is so, Rawls has not succeeded in showing that his favored principles are the ones that would be chosen behind the veil of ignorance and hence has not shown that his principles are correct solutions to the question of what justice is.

Rawls's theory also seems defective with respect to the idea that justice should reflect contribution or effort. Imagine a society made up of two people organized according to Rawls's favored fundamental principles. Suppose one person lies around doing as little as possible while the other goes to work creating tools to produce more in the future. When that future comes, must the hardworking person share the increased wealth produced by her efforts with the lazy idler? The difference principle would seem to require that at least some benefit go to the lazy person, but this does not seem to be just.

Another problem with Rawls's theory of justice is that it is not sensitive to the different needs that people have. Rawls's theory considers only which differences in income are acceptable. But two people with the same income may have radically different needs. A society might be just in a Rawlsian sense and yet award the same share of resources to people with radically different needs.

A number of philosophers have tried to correct these defects of Rawls's theory from within the Rawlsian framework of thinking of justice in terms of fundamental rules that would be chosen by rational individuals from behind a veil of ignorance. James Sterba, for example, has argued in favor of a guaranteed minimum income with no other restrictions on inequalities as preferable to Rawls's difference principle. Sterba argues that this avoids the risks inherent in the utilitarian strategy and at the same time avoids the difference principle's insensitivity to effort and contribution that requires that gains produced by hard workers be shared with lazy idlers.[12] In two important articles another philosopher, Ronald Dworkin, addressed both the problem of the person unfairly disadvantaged by natural circumstances and the problem of the lazy idler, developing an elaborate scheme that involves from behind the veil of ignorance both an auction of all available resources and purchases of more or less expensive insurance policies that will compensate those individuals who find themselves in the actual postcontract world filling the positions of those disadvantaged by natural misfortune.[13]

Space does not permit the further reflection these proposals deserve. For our purposes it will have to suffice here to note that, like Rawls's theory and the other theories of justice examined in this chapter, these proposals aim to articulate a conception of what a just distribution of wealth would be. They do so by trying to indicate what features of a just world ought and ought not to affect one's income. In this sense, each tries to identify a pattern that serves as the template for an ideally just distribution of wealth. In the next chapter we will look at a radical challenge to any such conception of justice.

## —— Chapter 7 ——

# The Libertarian Challenge

Theories of distributive justice of the kind we have been considering hold that justice consists in finding a distributive outcome that conforms to some ideal pattern of how income and wealth should be distributed. These theories differ about what that ideal pattern is. Some say that income should correspond to contribution, others say that it should correspond to effort or need, and still others say that it should correspond to a more abstract criterion such as the maximization of average utility or the distribution specified by Rawls's difference principle. In an important book published in 1974, Robert Nozick offered a radical challenge to any such "patterned" theory of justice.[1]

In the real world, of course, it is highly unlikely that any society would ever achieve a distribution of income that would perfectly match the ideal pattern stipulated by some philosophical theory of distributive justice. But, just for the sake of argument, suppose that some society somewhere did do just that. This society has achieved a state of perfect justice in distribution, and accordingly each individual in this society is justly entitled to hold the income that he or she holds. Now a disturbing thing happens. Michael Jordan, having retired from professional basketball, offers to play exhibition basketball for the public in exchange for a $2 admission fee.[2] Millions of fans are delighted at the chance to see Jordan play again and consider the admission fee a real bargain. Each of these fans pays for his admission fee out of his own, on our own view, just holdings. But the resultant distribution of wealth, involving the transfer of millions of dollars from the fans to Michael Jordan, violates the perfect pattern of justice that had been achieved. Must we then deny that the fans and Jordan had a right to enter into their mutually satisfying agreement?

Must we, in the name of distributive justice, "forbid capitalist acts between consenting adults?"[3]

Any pattern of distribution, once achieved, is likely to be upset by acts of individuals with respect to the dispersement of the income they hold. A harmless gift between lovers would lead from a distribution satisfying the pattern of justice to a distribution not satisfying that pattern. Hence, any patterned theory of justice seems to require an extensive and continuous interference with the liberty of individuals to do with their income what they like. Liberty upsets patterns, and any political philosophy that attempts to realize on earth some ideal pattern of justice will be forced to pervasively interfere with the liberty of individual persons. Libertarianism, the political philosophy defended by Nozick, rejects any such interference with individual liberty. It is a political philosophy based on the consistent and inviolable defense of individual liberty as the fundamental principle of all political and social life.

## Liberalism and Liberty

The libertarian challenge to theories of distributive justice can serve as the basis for a reexamination of the place of liberty in the liberal tradition. There can be no doubt that liberals, both classical and new, have always proclaimed their love of liberty, but the libertarian challenge raises deep concerns about the centrality of liberty in the liberal vision and the strength of the philosophical commitment to liberty within liberalism.

Within classical liberalism, liberty was understood as negative freedom, as the absence of interference with the individual. John Stuart Mill's great defense of liberty in *On Liberty* clearly had such a negative conception of liberty in mind. The harm principle, which Mill claims should rightly govern all relations between the individual and society, says that "the sole end for which mankind are warranted, individually or collectively, in interfering with the liberty of action of any of their number, is self-protection."[4] As we have seen, by "self-protection" Mill means the prevention of harm to other people. So long as an individual's action harms no one else, Mill argues that society may not interfere with that individual. Noninterference, or negative freedom, is thus the central idea of liberty in the Mill's classical liberalism.

In contrast, as we have seen, new liberals championed a positive conception of freedom, defined by T.H. Green as "a positive power or capacity of doing or enjoying something worth doing or enjoying."[5] In the view of Green and the new liberals who followed his philosophical lead, freedom understood as the mere absence of interference by other people is not sufficient. For the new liberals, just as a negative freedom of movement is useless to a paraplegic who lacks the resources to get around, so too negative freedom without resources is empty for the poor and socially disadvantaged. In this way the new liberals sought to bring a concern for improving the lot of the poor and disadvantaged within the compass of the traditional liberal concern for freedom.

Mirroring the distinction between negative freedom and positive freedom is a distinction between negative rights and positive rights. As we have seen, classical liberalism incorporated into its conception of how political and social life should be organized the array of individual rights proclaimed by the American and French revolutionaries on the basis of their theories of natural law and natural rights. Liberals, even those who followed the dominant utilitarian thinking in rejecting the ideas of natural law and natural rights, believed that in a good society the primary function of government was the protection of such rights.

For the most part, these rights can be understood as negative rights. That is, they are rights against the interference of other people or the interference of governments in our lives. Thus, for example, understood as negative rights, the right to life is a right not to be killed, and the right to liberty is a right not to be enslaved, imprisoned, or in any way held captive against one's will. The Bill of Rights, consisting of the first ten amendments to the Constitution of the United States, lists the familiar freedoms of religion, speech, press, assembly, and so on as rights that belong to the people and upon which the government may not infringe. Understood as the freedom to practice one's religion, to speak and write as one likes, and to assemble with others, all without interference by any other person, these rights are negative rights.

But, just as the new liberals added positive freedoms to negative freedoms, so too they added positive rights to negative rights. While negative rights are rights not to be interfered with, positive rights are rights to have some resource provided that is deemed necessary to living a morally acceptable form of life. Rights to education, housing, and medical care are all examples of such positive rights. They demand not just that governments and other individuals refrain from interference, but that positive steps be taken to provide schools, housing, and medical care to those who are too poor to provide them for themselves.

In the long period during which the philosophy of the new liberalism dominated thinking in most of the advanced industrial countries, from the closing decades of the nineteenth century until the 1970s, it was taken for granted by most political philosophers, and most practicing politicians, that securing positive freedoms and positive rights were the legitimate aims of good government. The "Four Freedoms" proclaimed by the administration of Franklin D. Roosevelt in 1942 included alongside the negative freedoms of speech and worship a clearly positive "freedom from want." And the same planning document that proclaimed this freedom from want also listed a "new bill of rights" that included positive rights to food, clothing, shelter, medical care, rest, and recreation.[6] Similar commitments to positive freedoms and positive rights can be found in the United Nations Universal Declaration of Human Rights, adopted in 1948, and in many other national and international documents concerning human rights and the rights of citizens.[7]

We have already seen how the new liberalism's extension of liberalism to include positive freedom and positive rights disturbed some of those thinkers who claimed allegiance to classical liberalism and its understanding of freedom and rights in terms of negative freedom and negative rights. In their view, the use of the concepts of positive freedom and positive rights to justify an increasingly large and increasingly intrusive welfare state marked a dangerous betrayal of classical liberalism's commitment to individual liberty. A.V. Dicey, a distinguished English legal scholar and a follower of the classical liberalism of James Mill during the middle of the nineteenth century, became a sharp critic of the new liberalism by the end of the century. Writing in 1896, Dicey pointed out that T.H. Green's positive definition of freedom was "unnatural" and that it lent support to a growing current of state intervention in the affairs of individuals and to "social despotism."[8] In a similar vein, in "From Freedom to Bondage," an essay published in 1891, the classical liberal Herbert Spencer attacked the new liberalism for its betrayal of liberty.[9]

Similar criticisms of new liberalism as the enemy of liberty surfaced here and there throughout the long hegemony of new liberal philosophy. Prominent among these critics were F.A. Hayek, who argued in *The Road to Serfdom* that new liberal dreams of using the power of the state to eliminate poverty and injustice threaten individual liberty, and Milton Friedman, who argued in *Capitalism and Freedom* that the growing welfare state posed a threat to individual liberty.[10] One might also mention here the many books of the novelist and essayist Ayn Rand, who vividly portrayed the totalitarian implications of Communism in her native Russia and championed individual liberty against the claims of government, society, and other individuals.[11] Each of these thinkers shared the idea that the welfare state threatened individual liberty and each contributed to the critique of the new liberalism and to the development of libertarianism as an alternative to new liberalism in political philosophy.

Classical liberalism was born of the confluence of natural-rights theory and utilitarianism, with utilitarianism gaining ascendancy by early nineteenth century. For the most part, liberal thinkers followed Bentham in viewing the ideas of natural law and natural rights as "metaphysical" concepts, not verifiable by any experiential test, and tainted with theological presuppositions. Utilitarianism, which made no theological assumptions and dealt with the experientially confirmable states of human pain and pleasure, appeared more acceptable to the scientific outlook that came increasingly to dominate modern thought. Unfortunately, that utilitarianism provided at best only a shaky foundation for liberty and the rights of individuals championed by classical liberalism.

As we have seen, in *On Liberty* John Stuart Mill explicitly relinquishes "any advantage which could be derived to my argument from the idea of abstract liberty," and bases his case for liberty on the grounds that liberty is conducive to happiness.[12] In a similar way, Adam Smith argues for freedom of trade on the grounds that free markets will maximize the wealth of nations and, consequently, the total amount of happiness produced. For utilitarians such as Mill and Smith, liberty is valuable only as a means to happiness; liberty has extrinsic value but not intrinsic value. While the arguments offered by Smith and Mill are powerful ones, resting on broad appeals to human nature, social science, and human experience, they leave room for possible abridgments of liberty.

For example, one might argue, as does a character in Dostoyevsky's novel *The Brothers Karamazov,* that ultimately liberty brings greater suffering to human beings than they are able to bear. Were this true, the consistent utilitarian would have to abandon liberty, since for the utilitarian it is happiness, not liberty, that is the ultimate goal of political philosophy.

Such a wholesale abandonment of liberty was never a part of the thinking of the new liberalism. Indeed, leading new liberals such as Green, Hobhouse, and Dewey remained as convinced as Mill and Smith that there was a strong connection between liberty and happiness. Nevertheless, because they viewed liberty as a means to happiness, in principle they were willing to sacrifice specific claims to liberty where doing so could be shown to actually contribute to maximizing happiness. In particular, the new liberals were willing to restrict the liberty of property owners to do what they wanted with the property they owned in order to advance the positive freedoms of workers, and to tax the rich to support programs aimed at helping the poor for the sake of advancing the welfare of society as a whole. For utilitarians, the commitment to liberty was not absolute, but only conditional on liberty's conduciveness to happiness. For a political philosophy such as libertarianism, which makes an inviolable commitment to individual liberty its fundamental principle, utilitarianism is an unreliable ally.

## Rights-Based Theories

In the very first sentence of *Anarchy, State, and Utopia,* Robert Nozick says, "Individuals have rights, and there are things no person or group may do to them (without violating their rights). So strong and far-reaching are these rights that they raise the question of what, if anything, the state and its officials may do."[13] The rights that Nozick claims here are not rights that are created by any government or any human agency. In this sense, they are natural rights, rights that human beings have simply in virtue of their existence as human beings. Among the rights central to Nozick's view is the right to liberty, a right to do what one wants with one's life without interference from government or any other person so long as one's actions do not interfere with the like liberty of others.

Nozick believes that the right to liberty forms a "side constraint" on what governments or other people may do. Suppose there is something the government would like to do that would greatly increase the total happiness of society as a whole but which involves violating my right to liberty. In saying that my right to liberty is a side constraint, Nozick means that it blocks any such governmental project. My right to liberty may not be violated even if doing so would achieve greater overall happiness. Further, suppose some dictator agrees to release a hundred political prisoners on the grounds that you capture me and turn me over to him to be his prisoner. By capturing me and achieving the release of the hundred political prisoners, you would maximize nonviolations of the right to liberty. But by calling the right to liberty a side constraint, Nozick means to prohibit even this. My right to liberty may not be violated even if doing so minimizes total violations of rights to liberty. My right to liberty is, in a sense, an absolute right, not violable for any reason.

This idea of a strong right to liberty, understood as a negative right not to be interfered with that belongs to every normal adult human being and which may not be violated to achieve some other purpose, is fundamental to libertarian political philosophy. For the libertarian, this absolute or near-absolute right to liberty is the cornerstone upon which the edifice of economic, social, and political institutions must be built. In an essay published in 1974, "What Libertarianism Is," the libertarian philosopher John Hospers says, "Every human being has the right to act in accordance with his own choices, unless those actions infringe on the equal liberty of other human beings to act in accordance with *their* choices."[14] In a later essay with the same title Hospers says that, "The essential ingredient in all this is freedom from coercion by others. This is one's basic and inalienable right."[15] The libertarian philosopher Jan Narveson makes an even stronger claim about the centrality of the right to liberty, saying that "the only relevant consideration in political matters is individual liberty."[16]

Unlike utilitarianism, which makes the right to liberty a means to the end of social happiness, libertarianism conceives of the right to liberty as an independent foundation for political philosophy. It, not the maximization of happiness nor any other end, is the "bottom line" for political philosophy. Further, in conceiving of the right to liberty as inviolable, as a side constraint on all other economic, social, and political institutions, libertarians raise the independently grounded right to liberty above all other considerations. For these reasons, libertarianism is said to be a "rights-based" theory. In this respect, and in its conception of the right to liberty as one belonging to human beings by nature and not by human convention, libertarianism agrees with the older natural-rights tradition and disagrees with utilitarianism.

This shift away from utilitarianism to rights-based theories was characteristic of a broad movement in ethics and political philosophy in the 1960s and 1970s. This shift was largely motivated by imagined cases that seemed to show that utilitarian principles led to morally unacceptable conclusions. In chapter 6 we considered the case of the utilitarian surgeon faced with five patients needing transplants and one patient whose organs happened to provide the needed matches for the five needing transplants. Utilitarianism, consistently applied, would seem to require the surgeon to painlessly kill the one in order to harvest organs for the five, thereby maximizing the total amount of happiness in the world, but also grossly violating our sense that such an action would be a morally unacceptable violation of individual rights. Faced with a number of such examples, most philosophers have come to the conclusion that utilitarianism is not tenable as a fundamental theory of morality, and consequently not tenable as the foundation for political philosophy. Though utilitarians have mounted some interesting defenses of their position, most philosophers have felt that these defenses ultimately fail and have turned to rights-based theories or mixed theories as more adequately accounting for our fundamental moral judgments.[17]

As a rights-based theory, libertarianism built upon this shift away from utilitarianism in ethics and political theory. However, libertarianism represents only one current within the wider family of rights-based theories. Rawls's theory of justice, for example, also lies, broadly speaking, within the family of rights-based theories. Utilitarianism is often called a teleological or consequentialist theory. Such theories identify some quality or state of affairs as what is intrinsically good and then define morally right actions as those actions that aim at maximization of this good. In the case of utilitarianism, the good is happiness and right action is action that maximizes happiness. In contrast, Rawls's theory is a deontological theory, one that determines the rightness or wrongness of an action in terms of the kind of action that it is, and not in terms of the conduciveness of that action to the maximization of some good. Thus, for example, according to Rawls's theory, any suppression of liberty is morally wrong. In this, Rawls too accepts a strong right to liberty.[18] Other political philosophers have also supported the shift from utilitarianism to rights-based theories but do not adopt libertarian positions.

One characteristic of libertarians is that they reject claims to positive rights. We will examine the implications of this position more fully below. Here it suffices to note that the shift from utilitarianism to rights-based theories need not include the rejection of positive rights. Nor need the rights-based theorist agree with the libertarian that negative rights always override other moral and political considerations. For example, the philosopher Michael Freeden presents a complex theory that includes negative rights, positive rights, and considerations of utility.[19] Libertarianism is a particular current within the broader family of postutilitarian rights-based theories. It is, in a sense, a radical rights-based theory, one that challenges much of the fabric of law and practice that has come to govern economic, social, and political life in developed industrial societies. Having seen how libertarianism makes the right to liberty the cornerstone of political philosophy, it is to these radical implications of libertarian theory that we now turn.

## The Radical Implications of Libertarian Theory

Libertarians reject all positive rights. At the heart of libertarian theory is the right to liberty that belongs to every normal adult human being. Libertarians understand this right as a negative right, a right not to be interfered with in the conduct of one's life so long as one does not interfere with others in the free conduct of their lives. The libertarian understands this noninterference in terms of the absence of coercion. If I am walking down the street and a tourist from out of town stops me and asks for directions, there is a sense in which the tourist has interfered with me. By stopping me and asking for directions, the tourist interrupts the flow of my life. But I remain free to ignore this request. If I am in a hurry, or lost in thought, or just don't want to be bothered, I am free to go on my way. So far the libertarian has no objection to the actions of the tourist. But were the tourist to grab me by the arm and prevent my moving on, or threaten me with a gun and demand an answer, then the intervention of the tourist takes on a coercive aspect that aims at removing my freedom. It is such coercive intervention that the libertarian sees as interfering with my liberty in a morally objectionable way. Libertarians argue that positive rights inherently involve such coercive interference with liberty. To see why this is so, we must briefly consider the libertarian view of property rights.

To have a right of property in or over some thing is to have the right to use the thing; the right to sell, bequeath, or give away the thing; and the right to prevent others from using the thing. In this way, property rights are often said to be bundles of rights over objects. Now, each of these rights can be understood as involving a right of liberty with respect to the thing. To say that I have a right to use the thing is to say that I am free to use the thing and others may not coercively interfere to prevent me from using it. In the same way, to say that I have the rights to sell, bequeath, and give away the thing, is to say that I have a right of liberty to do these things that prevents others from coercively interfering in my doing so. And, finally, to say that I have a right to prevent others from using the thing is to say that the question of whether or not others may use the thing is one that falls within the domain of my free choice. You may not take my car without my consent. Your use of my car is up to me. It is a matter of my free choice. In this way the exercise of property rights over things that we own can be understood as inherent in our right to liberty. It is for this reason that for the government to forbid the basketball fans from spending their own money to see Michael Jordan play exhibition basketball appears to be a violation of liberty. Similar reasoning will also show that the right to life, understood as the right not to be killed, is also implicit in the right to liberty. After all, to kill someone is to coercively interfere with that person's freedom to do with her life as she wants.

Given this understanding of property rights, and the view that the right to liberty is inviolable, the libertarian argument against positive rights is straightforward. Negative rights, such as the right to life, the right to liberty, and the right to property, require nothing more of me than noninterference with the possessor of those rights: I must not kill, enslave, or take what is not my own. Negative rights require nothing further from me. They do not take from me anything that is my own. On the other hand, positive rights, such as the rights to food, clothing, housing, education, and medical care, all require the provision of resources to people who need them. Who is to provide these resources? In practice, of course, it is governmental agencies, supported by taxpayers, that bear the responsibility for meeting those needs. But taxpayers are not free to decline to pay their taxes. The government has a coercive power over individual taxpayers. Refusal to pay will be met with fines, imprisonment, and the forced confiscation of property. This is the fundamental difference between public assistance and private charity from the libertarian's point of view. Donations to private charities are voluntary donations. They are given without coercive intervention or the threat of coercive intervention. Taxes, on the other hand, are extracted under a coercive threat. Positive rights claim rights to the provision of resources. But if A has a right to X, then B or someone else, must provide X. The provision of X has ceased to be B's voluntary contribution.

The case against positive rights is neatly summed up in this passage from Ayn Rand:

> Jobs, food, clothing, recreation, homes, medical care, education, etc. do not grow in nature. They are man-made values—goods and services produced by men. *Who* is to provide them?
>
> If some men are entitled *by right* to the products of the work of others, it means that those others are deprived of rights and condemned to slave labor.
>
> Any alleged right of one man, which necessitates the violation of the rights of another, is not and cannot be a right.
>
> No one can have a right to impose an unchosen obligation, an unrewarded duty or an involuntary servitude on another man. There can be no such thing as *the right to enslave.*
>
> A right does not include the material implementation of that right by others; it includes only the freedom to earn that implementation by one's own effort.[20]

The argument is simple and powerful. Since positive rights inherently require the provision of resources, they inherently violate the freedom of at least some persons by requiring those persons to pay whether they want to or not.

The libertarian's rejection of positive rights has broad implications. Under the sway of new liberal thinking, more or less extensive welfare states were constructed in all of the advanced industrial countries. Typically, governments have supplied resources to provide food, shelter, education, and medical care to persons in need. All of these things are financed by taxation. In a libertarian society, all such programs would be eliminated and would be replaced by private, voluntary charities. A libertarian society would even do away with many public services that antedate new liberalism. There are a number of other services paid for by coercive taxation that are not directly targeted at poor people. For example, in the United States, public schools and public highways are financed by taxation and have been for the entire history of the republic. In a libertarian society none of these things would be provided by governmental agencies. All would be privatized and paid for by those who use these services. Also gone from a libertarian society would be public support for art, science, and recreation. Museums, libraries, and parks would be privatized and financed by fees assessed upon those who use them. In short, from the central claim of an inviolable right to liberty, libertarian philosophy reaches conclusions that would require radical changes in how we have traditionally understood the public realm and the proper role of government.

Libertarian philosophy also requires a radical change in how we view trade unions. As we have seen, during the hegemony of the new liberalism, trade unions gained the power to force employers to bargain collectively with employees in entering into contracts governing wages and terms of employment. From a libertarian point of view, this is an unacceptable interference with the rights of liberty of employers and employees alike. Libertarians have no objection to trade unions. Workers may voluntarily join any organization they like so long as they do not attempt to use that organization to impose their will contrary to the liberty of others. Employers are also free to bargain with unions if they choose to do so. What the libertarian finds objectionable is not the existence of unions or collective bargaining, but the existence of a body of law that compels employers to bargain with unions. Here the right to liberty of the employer is clearly violated. The libertarian also finds objectionable any attempt by unions to impose their will on workers who, for whatever reason, choose not to join a union or go along with a union action. If a union chooses to strike, the libertarian has no objection. Workers are free men, not slaves. They have the right not to enter into a contract with their employers. But if a union does strike, its members may not impose their will on employees who want to work. If a strike is called and other people, either former employees or outsiders, desire to enter into a contract on terms acceptable to the employer, the union does not have any right to try to prevent these other people from working. From the libertarian perspective, violence, threats of violence, and intimidating picketing all involve unacceptable violations of the liberty of those people who do want to work. Here too, libertarian philosophy would require a radical change in the laws that have been developed regarding unions, the obligation of employers to bargain with unions, and the right, in some countries and in some states of the United States, for unions to organize closed shops, which legally exclude non–union members from employment.[21]

## A Libertarian Theory of Justice

We began this chapter with consideration of Robert Nozick's libertarian critique of patterned theories of distributive justice. We saw how any attempt to maintain some ideal pattern of distribution must necessarily violate the liberty of individuals. Now, with some understanding of the core ideas of libertarianism, we can ask what a libertarian theory of justice regarding the distribution of wealth and income would look like. In a sense, the answer to this question is that a just distribution of wealth and income might look just about any way, according to libertarian principles. The key thing about the libertarian theory of justice is that it does not aim at preserving any pattern at all. For the libertarian, any pattern of distribution is just provided it arises in a morally acceptable way. Let us suppose that some initial distribution of property exists and that it is just. We will return to this matter of the initial distribution of property in the next chapter, but for now, assume that some just initial distribution exists. Now each person owns some property. Accordingly, each person has the right to keep, sell, trade, bequeath, or give this property away, and no one may coercively intervene to prevent the owner from doing anything he or she chooses with it. Now, suppose a sequence of sales, trades, bequeathments, and gifts takes place and that each of these transfers is freely done without any coercive intervention. From a libertarian point of view, each of these transfers is morally acceptable. This being so, since by hypothesis the initial distribution of property was also just, the libertarian argues that it follows that the resulting distribution of property is just. From this perspective what counts is not the nature of the end pattern of distribution, but the moral purity of the history by which this end distribution is reached. In *Anarchy, State, and Utopia,* Nozick defends this "historical" conception of justice against all patterned theories of justice. Unlike the various patterned theories, such a historical conception is consistent with the strong right to individual liberty championed by Nozick and his libertarian allies.

A number of very interesting problems remain. Among these is the problem of how to specify what makes for justice with respect to any possible initial distribution of resources. However, we shall postpone consideration of this and other difficulties to the following chapter. Here our aim has been only to understand what libertarians say, some of the considerations that lead them to say these things, and the implications of libertarians' ideas.

# Chapter 8

# Answering the Libertarian Challenge

While nowhere on this earth does there exist a truly libertarian society, libertarian ideas have been internationally influential in the closing decades of the twentieth century. Under the charismatic leadership of Margaret Thatcher in Britain and Ronald Reagan in the United States, libertarian ideas have influenced public policy in two of the most powerful nations in the world. Libertarian thinking has also played a role in reshaping the societies of the former Communist world and in laying the foundations for the "new world order" proclaimed by former U.S. president George Bush, a new world order built upon the foundations of free trade and respect for human rights. In addition, libertarian ideas have contributed to institutional changes in the areas of criminal justice and the provision of welfare services, supporting programs that emphasize personal responsibility and retribution for wrongdoing. Libertarianism has also provided support for privatization of public services, public utilities, public schools, and public pension plans. While no reasonable person would claim that these changes in the political currents of the times are directly due to libertarian philosophy, it would be equally unreasonable to suppose that the flowering of libertarian philosophy in the 1970s and 1980s has been without any influence on the course of events. In any case, however much libertarian ideas may have contributed to the political currents of the times, as philosophical ideas, they are worthy of serious attention. Libertarianism offers a relatively clear, coherent, and powerful conception of how societies ought to be organized. Its strong central commitment to individual liberty and individual rights cannot but appeal to us who, living at the end of the twentieth century, know of the horrors of the gulag and the Holocaust.[1] Still, libertarianism is not without its difficulties. Having in the previous chapter developed a sense of what libertarianism says, in this chapter we will examine some of these difficulties.

## The Metaphysics of Rights

Libertarianism is a rights-based theory. It bases itself on a strong conception of rights that human beings have independent of any consideration of utility or the collective good of the society as a whole. Further, according to the libertarian, these rights are natural in the sense that they do not depend upon any human agency and cannot be taken away by any human agency. This conception of human rights as natural is one libertarians share with Locke and the other great thinkers of the natural-law and natural-rights tradition. But, as we have seen already, Bentham and the utilitarians subjected the ideas of natural law and natural rights to a withering criticism. According to Bentham, claims about natural rights were metaphysically suspect. Such rights were strange entities, not detectable by the scientific methods of observation and reason based on observation. Because claims to have such rights were untestable and unprovable, they were, on Bentham's view, "nonsense," empty words without meaning or significance. The conservative philosopher Edmund Burke concurred with Bentham in this at least, dismissing the proclamations of rights by American and French revolutionaries as subjective products of human fantasy.[2] How might the libertarian defend the notion of natural rights against such criticisms?

There are a number of lines of argument open to the libertarian here. Actually, Bentham and Burke ignored at least one promising line of defense for claims to natural rights. As we saw in chapter 1, natural-rights theorists thought that claims about rights could be derived from observation and reason. By observation we learn that it is in the nature of knives to have sharp edges. By observation we learn that such an edge is conducive to cutting and is damaged by use as a pry bar. By reason we conclude that the right way to use a knife is for cutting and that to use a knife to pry nails is a misuse of it, a use contrary to its nature. In the same way we learn by observation that human beings have a capacity for autonomous self-direction, for forming goals and plans to reach those goals. Accordingly, to enslave a person is to misuse him, to use him contrary to his nature. Human beings have a natural right to liberty because liberty conforms to human nature, to the natural capacity humans have to form their own life plans and act accordingly.

But there is a problem with this argument. The argument moves from claims about the nature of a thing to conclusions about how we ought to treat the thing. Because human beings have the capacity for autonomous self-direction, we ought to respect their liberty of action. But there is a logical lacuna here. From claims about what is the case, nothing follows about what should be the case.[3] I might, for example, acknowledge that humans have the capacity for self-direction but hold that this is an evil trait in them that ought to be suppressed. Arguments for natural rights rest upon the suppressed premise that we ought to treat things in accordance with their natures. Given this premise, and the claim that humans have by nature a capacity for autonomous self-direction, it would follow that we ought to treat people in accordance with that capacity, that we ought not enslave them. But how can we prove the premise that we ought to treat things in accordance with their natures?

Locke and many of the natural-law theorists did have an answer here. Locke argued that God made us, that God does nothing in vain, and that accordingly God intends for humans to use their capacity for autonomous self-direction. But if this is so, then God intends for us not to interfere with other people so as to prevent their using this capacity. So far these premises speak only of what is the case. They tell us what human nature is and what God's intentions are. So far nothing has been said about what ought to be the case. But now Locke adds the premise that we ought to do what God wants. With this premise, Locke is able to bridge the gap between the "is" and the "ought."[4] But it is not a premise Bentham or the utilitarians were willing to accept. In their view, the need to have recourse to theology was a sign of the metaphysical and unscientific status of the natural-rights tradition.[5]

The modern libertarian John Hospers offers an alternative grounding of the central libertarian claim for a natural right to liberty. He holds that the right to liberty is a consequence of one's ownership of his own life:

> The political philosophy that is called libertarianism (from the Latin *libertas*, liberty) is the doctrine that every person is the owner of his own life, and that no one is the owner of anyone else's life; and that consequently every human being has the right to act in accordance with

his own choices, unless those actions infringe on the equal liberty of other human beings to act in accordance with *their* choices."[6]

This argument is clearly inadequate as an attempt to provide a general foundation for a theory of natural rights. In the first place, to say that everyone is the owner of his own life is to attribute a bundle of ownership rights over one's own life to each individual. But clearly this begs the question, assuming the existence of a natural right of ownership when it is the existence of such rights that is at issue. A philosopher such as Bentham, who questioned the whole idea of natural rights, would not be impressed by this argument.

There is also considerable room for doubt about the truth of the presupposed ownership rights, even assuming that some natural rights do exist. After all, it has long been a tenet of several of the world's great religions that our lives belong to God and not to ourselves. Other philosophers have held that our lives belong, at least in part, to our parents and to the community that nurtured us. In Plato's *Crito,* for example, Socrates seems to hold all of these positions, arguing that suicide is wrong because it amounts to stealing from the gods and that we owe a degree of obedience to our parents and the communities that have nurtured us.

Another libertarian strategy for supporting claims about the existence of rights draws on the resources of social-contract theory. Like Rawls, the libertarian asks us to imagine individuals entering into a social contract whereby they agree to live together according to certain fundamental rules. The libertarian argues that it is in the self-interest of each to adopt inviolable rights to life, liberty, and property as fundamental rules governing social life. While by doing so each loses the freedom to act aggressively against the others, each gains security against the aggression of others. Since such security is necessary for just about any course of life a human being might happen to desire, each gains more by entering into this agreement than she loses by doing so. In this way fundamental rights can be grounded in the self-interest of rational individuals.[7]

But here too there are difficulties. While it is true that each individual is better off in a society where everyone respects rights to life, liberty, and property than she would be in a society where no one does so, each is even better off living in a society where everyone else respects those rights and she does not. It is in the self-interest of

Lucrezia to promise to respect basic rights and persuade others to do so also. But it may well be in her self-interest, when she is nearly certain she can get away with it, to break the promise she has made and poison her rich uncle. Further, each person who enters into the social contract on the basis of self-interest is in exactly the same position as Lucrezia. It is in the self-interest of each of us to agree to respect basic rights and yet to break this argument when it is to our advantage to do so. For this kind of reason, it is difficult to see how strong rights can be constructed on the basis of individual self-interest. Just as the principle of utility would seem to require the consistent utilitarian to defect from respecting rights in some situations, so rational self-interest would seem to require defection in some cases. Like utilitarianism, self-interest fails to provide a solid foundation for morally inviolable rights.

For the most part, Nozick is not concerned to prove that rights exist. He simply assumes that individuals have a strong right to liberty and explores the implications of this. However, in a section where Nozick explains his view of the right to liberty as a side constraint against coercive interference, he suggests that such an inviolable right against coercion rests on Kantian moral theory: "Side constraints upon action reflect the underlying Kantian principle that individuals are ends and not merely means; they may not be sacrificed or used for the achieving of other ends without their consent."[8] It is certainly true that the Kantian principle, insofar as it sets constraints on how people may be treated no matter what the end in view may be, seems to provide support for a rights-based political philosophy. But the Kantian principle, at least as developed by Kant, itself rests upon dubious metaphysical foundations.

As we noted in chapter 6, Kant held that human beings are metaphysically different from mere things. Insofar as we are viewed as parts of the natural universe, everything about us is causally determined. Were this the whole story about us, in Kant's view we would not be morally responsible for our actions and would not have the peculiar quality of rational practical agency that elevates us above other animals and objects, making of us ends that may not be treated as mere means. In short, Kant's defense of rights rests on a metaphysics that rejects naturalism. For him, human beings are contained within the natural order only insofar as we concern ourselves with the phenomenal world of appearances. The true nature of human beings lies hidden in the world of things in themselves. Now it may be that Kant is wrong in thinking that naturalism precludes responsibility and that the Kantian principle is reconcilable with naturalism, but it is not obvious that this is so. In any case, the libertarian who embraces the whole of Kant takes on considerable metaphysical difficulties, and the libertarian who wants to extract the moral principle from its surrounding Kantian metaphysics needs to show that this is possible.

Perhaps in the end the best approach for the libertarian to take is to simply assume that certain rights do exist. Most of us are prepared to follow the libertarian in postulating inviolable or nearly inviolable rights to life and liberty. However, a much greater controversy surrounds the libertarian view that each individual also has a strong right to property. Let us now turn to consideration of some of the difficulties faced by the libertarian with regard to such a right to property. Does the libertarian have good reason to think that every individual has a right to property? Is the right to property inviolable or nearly so? Is taxation to pay for entitlements claimed by positive rights a violation of individuals' rights? These are some of the questions we will be considering.

### Libertarian Property Rights: A Critical Assessment

Libertarians often compare taxation to support welfare safety nets with armed robbery, slavery, and forced-labor camps. Since taxation is backed up by the coercive power of government, it is viewed as morally equivalent in kind to the coercive power of the thief, the slave-holder, and the dictator. Such a view rests upon the assumption that people have strong rights over the property that they own, rights that are somehow essentially connected with the right to liberty, so that taxation and slavery are essentially the same. Do we have such rights? What is the connection between property rights over things and the individual's right to liberty? How do we come to have property rights over things?

#### *The Problem Of Original Acquisition*

Suppose we were to trace the ownership history of some piece of property, either in land or in some other kind of good. The object will have a history of transfers from one owner to another. These transfers may involve sale, trade, gift, or bequeathment, for example. The history of an object may also involve some process of manufacture, where the manufacturer purchases raw materials and combines them to form a finished product, which is then sold to a customer. All of these transfers involve a change in ownership rights from one person to another. But how did anyone ever first come to own anything? If we trace the ownership of any object backward in time, eventually we must reach a point where land, or ore, or trees, or some other natural product that was not owned by any human being comes to be owned by someone. Strong property rights of the kind envisaged by the libertarian give the owner of the thing complete control over the thing, control that includes the right to prevent others from using the thing without permission of the owner. How can this be? How can some individual come to have exclusive rights over a part of the world that previously was not owned by anyone at all? The idea that individual human beings can somehow acquire ownership rights over parts of the earth has struck many people as strange. Many of the native American peoples believed that the land belonged to the people as a whole for their use. A similar view, that the earth belonged in usufruct to the living, was held by Thomas Jefferson as well.[9]

This problem of original acquisition is important for the libertarian in at least two ways. First, according to Nozick's libertarian theory of justice, the justice of any distribution of goods is a function of the history of that distribution rather than of the pattern exhibited by that distribution. If the distribution was reached by just transfers from justly acquired initial holdings, then and only then is the distribution just. This account needs some theory of justice in original acquisition. Second, libertarian complaints that taxation to support welfare safety nets is slavery requires property rights of a very strong kind, rights that are not in any way encumbered by social obligations. But since transfer can only transfer rights previously acquired, the libertarian is going to need some account of original acquisition that yields strong property rights of the kind presupposed by the criticism of taxation for social welfare programs. Can the libertarian deliver?

In chapter 4, in considering the anarchist Proudhon's claim that "property is theft," we briefly considered the account of original acquisition offered by John Locke. Locke argued that by mixing one's own labor with objects in their natural state, one comes to have a property right over the natural object. Some libertarians appear to have endorsed this Lockean account of original acquisition.[10] But other libertarians have rejected Locke's account for the reasons we noted in our discussion of it.[11] Briefly put, it is not clear why one gains a right over the entire object and not just over the portion of the worked object made up of the labor one mixed in.

Ayn Rand has suggested that property rights are derivable from the right to life. She argues that since material goods are necessary to sustain life, we have a right to possess them.[12] However, this suggestion ill serves the libertarian cause. In the first place, it fails to establish the strong kind of property rights necessary for libertarian criticisms of the welfare state, since it grounds rights over property only to the extent that we have need of that property to sustain life. Second, Rand's argument construes the right to life, and the derivative rights to material goods, as positive rights of the kind that libertarians reject. For the libertarian, the right to life, properly understood, is the negative right not to be killed, not the positive right to the material goods necessary to sustain life. Finally, Rand's argument reveals a deep fissure between her own ethical egoism, according to which the highest virtue consists in selfishness, in doing what is good for the self, and libertarianism, which puts respect for the rights of others on a moral par with pursuit of one's self-interest.

Having noted that "many writers seem to think that there is a terrible problem about extending a right of personal freedom to the use of items in the external world," Jan Narveson goes on dismiss the supposed problem: "Just as we can do what we wish with the natural parts of our own person, bodily and psychological, so we may do what we wish with bits of external nature, so long only as we do not thereby damage or impede the uses by others of such objects."[13] But, as stated here, Narveson's view amounts to nothing more than the mere assertion that, "just as" we have a right to liberty, so too we have property rights over bits of the external world. In particular, Narveson does not give us any reason for thinking that property rights over external objects are "extensions" of a right to personal freedom, in the sense of being somehow based on or derivable from the right to personal freedom. We will return to this question concerning the relationship between the right to liberty and property rights below. For now, let us focus on the restrictions on property rights mentioned by Narveson when he says that we may exercise control over bits of external nature "so long as we do not thereby damage or impede the uses by others of such objects."

Suppose you and I are hunter-gatherers living in proximity to one another. Suppose there is a section of woods that is particularly rich in wild fruit, berries, nuts, and small game. Now suppose I claim this woods as my own property and forbid you to forage for food there. But surely in doing so I damage or impede your use of the woods. After all, before I claimed it as my personal property, you were free to use it as you liked. Now, wouldn't this be true of all original acquisitions? Strong private property rights of the kind claimed by libertarians certainly do include the right of the owner to exclude others from use of the thing. So don't all original acquisitions damage or impede the use of the thing acquired by others?

This objection is not entirely fair to Narveson. What he says is that my claiming the woods as my own must not damage or impede your use of "such objects." To be sure, my claim impedes your use of this woods, but so long as there are plenty of other woods readily available to you, you retain access to "such objects." Here Narveson clearly has in mind a proviso that Locke attached to his own account of original acquisition: I am entitled to make a part of nature my own only if there be "enough and as good left in common for others."[14] The idea, then, is that I can make some part of nature my own private property so long as equally good portions of nature remain available for other people to use in common or claim as their own. If I were to claim the only source of water in the area as my own, I would be violating the proviso, while if I claim an acre of land, leaving plenty more available, I would not.

There is a certain reasonableness to the Lockean proviso. Clearly, if I claim the only source of water as my own, I seriously damage your interests in a way that I do not when I claim the single acre as my own, leaving you with ample land for your own use. But can the libertarian go along with Locke, as Narveson appears to do? Prior to any act of original acquisition you were at liberty to cross this piece of land. Now I claim this piece of land as my own. You are no longer at liberty to cross this piece of land. By my own unilateral action I have canceled your right to cross this piece of land. That there is as much and as good left over should not be relevant for the libertarian, for whom the right to liberty is inviolable.

There is also a regress problem that seems to render the Lockean proviso unsatisfiable. Nozick provides a clear formulation of the problem:

> Consider the first person Z for whom there is not enough and as good left to appropriate. The last person Y to appropriate left Z without his

previous liberty to act on an object, and so worsened Z's situation. So Y's appropriation is not allowed under Locke's proviso. Therefore the next to last person X to appropriate left Y in a worse position, for X's act ended permissible appropriation. Therefore X's appropriation wasn't permissible. But then the appropriator two from last, W, ended permissible appropriation and so, since it worsened X's position, W's appropriation wasn't permissible. And so on back to the first person A to appropriate a permanent property right.[15]

If satisfaction of the Lockean proviso is necessary for just acquisition, and if, as the regress argument seems to show, it cannot have been satisfied in the real world, where enough and as good is clearly not available for future appropriation, then it seems to follow that no actual property rights can be acceptable.

Having eloquently formulated this difficulty, Nozick claims to have found a way around it:

> Is the situation of persons who are unable to appropriate (there being no more accessible and useful unowned objects) worsened by a system allowing appropriation and permanent property? Here enter the various familiar social considerations favoring private property.... These considerations enter a Lockean theory to support the claim that appropriation of private property satisfies the intent behind the "enough and as good left over" proviso, *not* as a utilitarian justification of property. They enter to rebut the claim that because the proviso is violated no natural right to private property can arise by a Lockean process.[16]

The social considerations favoring private property Nozick has in mind here, omitted in the passage quoted above, will be considered below. They all have to do with the social benefits of private property, and they appear to provide a utilitarian case for private property. But Nozick insists that this is not their role here. His idea seems to be that since private property does have the kind of consequences claimed by the utilitarian argument, original acquisition does not leave even those for whom nothing is left to appropriate worse off than they would have been had there been no acquisition of private property.

But this interpretation of the Lockean proviso seems to countenance balancing lost liberties against opportunities and welfare gained. This is made especially clear in a footnote where Nozick speaks in terms of providing compensation only for those individuals "for whom the process of civilization was a *net loss,* for whom the benefits of civilization did not counterbalance being deprived of these particular liberties."[17] However reasonable, such a balancing seems flatly inconsistent with Nozick's own view of the right to liberty as a side constraint that may not be violated even for greater benefits.

It should also be noted that even if Nozick is successful in disarming the regress argument, what he has achieved in that case would be only to show that original acquisition has not been shown to be impermissible. We still do not have a libertarian account of how original acquisition is possible, and we certainly do not have a libertarian argument showing that private property rights are anything like direct extensions of the right to liberty. In the passage quoted above, Nozick talks about familiar social considerations favoring private property entering a "Lockean theory" to satisfy the restrictions imposed by the proviso, and just below the quoted passage he talks about private property arising by a "Lockean process." But the fact is that there is no "Lockean theory" or "Lockean process" remaining. The heart of the Lockean theory and the Lockean process was the idea of mixing one's labor with natural objects as the foundation for original acquisition. But Nozick himself has, rightly, rejected that idea. We are left, then, with no account of how original acquisition could produce strong property rights and no account of the supposed connection between liberty and property.

### On the Supposed Connection Between Liberty and Property

Libertarian comparisons of taxation with armed robbery, slavery, and forced labor reinforce the libertarian claim of an intimate connection between property rights and the right to liberty. Narveson makes an even stronger claim, holding that "liberty = property."[18] Narveson supports his claim in this way: "To own something is to have the right to do with it as one pleases: the disposition of that thing is up to you, not someone else." Now, if I have a right to do with something what I please, then I am free to do with that thing what I please. And if the disposition of the thing is entirely up to me and not to anyone else, then I am free to dispose of it as I see fit. And if I am free to do with or dispose of a thing solely as I see fit, then, perhaps, taxation would involve a violation of liberty, a violation of my freedom to dispose of my property as I see fit. But this argument works only if we assume that our property rights do give us the right to use or dispose of our property solely as we see fit. Do we have such strong property rights? Do we have the kinds of moral rights over the things that we own that Narveson claims that we do, or are our property rights in some way encumbered by social responsibilities? If property rights come with built-in social responsibilities, then we are not free to use and dispose of these things solely as we see fit, and taxation may exist without being a violation of our liberty.

Suppose Charlotte has a position as professor of Latin and Greek at Liberty College. Having this position, she has certain rights. She has, for example, the right to decide what books will be read in her classes and the right to say what she thinks about the matters of her expertise. Now, suppose Charlotte decides to sell her position to Harold, a retired fertilizer salesman with no training in classical languages. If the college intervenes to prevent Charlotte from selling the position to Harold, is it thereby violating her liberty to dispose of her property? If Liberty College requires Charlotte and all of its professors to give a final exam in her classes, is this "tax" on the available time for the course a violation of Charlotte's liberty?[19]

Of course, to have a college teaching position does not include the right to sell the position, and college teaching positions usually come with a number of institutional responsibilities attached. But this example does get us to see that "having" something may not be quite the all-or-nothing affair that Narveson's argument presupposes. Property rights are complex. Ownership of a thing typically brings with it a bundle of rights, including the rights to use and dispose of the thing claimed by Narveson. But, traditionally, property rights have also been thought to carry with them some responsibilities, including the responsibility of paying taxes. When I buy a house from you, I acquire the legal right to use the house and the legal right to dispose of it by selling it to someone else. But in buying the house I also acquire the legal responsibility of paying the property tax that has been assessed against that house. There is nothing mysterious about this. It would be decidedly odd for me to complain when the tax bill comes that the government is stealing my house. I knew about the legal encumbrance on the property when I bought it.

So much is obviously true if we consider the matter solely from a legal point of view. Narveson's complaint would be that the law is immoral in this respect. But this complaint rests upon the assumption that individuals hold moral rights over external things that do not carry with them moral responsibilities that may be morally enforced by governmental power, and Narveson has given us no reason for thinking that this assumption is true.

## *Property as an Adventitious Right*

Within the natural-rights tradition, many authors have distinguished between primary or primitive natural rights, which come to human beings directly from the hand of God, and secondary or adventitious natural rights, which depend upon human interpretations or applications of natural law. Among the primary natural rights are the rights to life and liberty that God gives to each individual human being, and the common right to use of the earth and all that it contains that God gave to humankind as a whole. Individual property rights, which assign particular parts of the external world to particular individuals, are understood as secondary or adventitious rights. A system of such rights is one way for human beings to make use of the earth that God gave in common to all human beings. This distinction between the primary natural rights of life and liberty and the adventitious rights of property can be found in the works of Grotius, Pufendorf, and Blackstone, among others, and may well have influenced Thomas Jefferson in his decision not to include the right to property as one of the fundamental human rights listed in the Declaration of Independence.[20]

Let us pursue this framework for regarding property rights a bit further. God has given us human beings the earth and all that it contains for our common use. Each of us needs food, clothing, and shelter to survive in this world, and each of us has wants for more goods than those necessary for mere survival. How shall we make use of our common heritage to satisfy our wants? We could organize ourselves communistically, regarding all natural resources and all that we produce from these resources as belonging not to individuals but to society as a whole. Or we could institute a system of private property, allowing individuals to claim parts of external nature as their own. Either of these approaches is a way in which we humans might share our common God-given heritage. Which system should we adopt? While it might appear that communism is closer to what God had in mind for us in giving the earth to us in common, considerations about the lack of individual incentives in communism, and the strong individual incentives associated with private ownership, might persuade reasonable people that a system of private property would be adventitious to us in trying to satisfy as many of our wants as possible. However, recognizing that God gave the earth to us in common, and recognizing the relative weakness of charity in the human soul, we would want to be sure to arrange our system of private property in such a way that individual property rights were linked with individual responsibilities to maintain the common good and to respect the natural right to liberty God gave to every human individual.

Here, then, is a way of understanding how human beings could have come to acquire private property consistent with natural rights to life and liberty. But it is important to note that the individual property rights produced in this way are not the strong property rights presupposed by libertarians.

## A Pseudolibertarian Argument

Since the time of Adam Smith, numerous thinkers have stressed the benefits that free markets bring to humankind. Similar arguments can be made for private property. Relevant here are those social considerations on behalf of private property mentioned by Nozick in the passage quoted above. Private property gives each owner an incentive to care for her property and utilize it in the most efficient way possible. Private property encourages experimentation and innovation, which ultimately benefits consumers. Private property allows individuals greater control over the level of risk to which they are exposed. And private property protects individual liberty by providing means of existence that are not controlled by central political powers. These arguments have been powerfully developed by important thinkers such as Ludwig von Mises, Friedrich Hayek, and Milton Friedman.[21] They are arguments deserving of attention, arguments that may well support the desirability of extensive rights to private property. But they are not libertarian arguments. For the most part, they are straightforwardly utilitarian arguments. They justify private property on the grounds that it has optimal consequences for maximizing the satisfaction of human wants. These are not rights-based arguments of the kind needed by libertarian theory. To be sure, there is no contradiction in being a libertarian and thinking that private property maximizes happiness. But one cannot make the supposed consequence of happiness maximization the grounds for a libertarian conception of property rights. Some other argument would be needed for that. Insofar as we make conduciveness to maximizing happiness the justification for private property, we leave room for considerations of distributive justice of the kind advanced by the new liberals—considerations that libertarian theory seeks to preclude.

## Workers' Rights

Libertarians oppose legally enforced collective bargaining, minimum-wage laws, government-imposed health and safety regulations, legally imposed limits on the working day, and other measures advocated by socialists and new liberals. They oppose these measures on the grounds that they interfere with the rights of private property, and consequently with the right to liberty. But this argument works only if we presuppose that individuals who do own property have complete and morally unencumbered control over the property that they own. A central argument in this chapter has been that libertarians have not succeeded in showing that individuals do have any such strong property rights. If individual property rights are adventitious rights, rights resulting from human-made arrangements for using our common, God-given heritage, there is some reason to think that individual property rights would not be so strong. The view of property rights as adventitious understands them as rights that must come encumbered with communally enforceable moral responsibilities. If God gave us the earth as our common heritage, any way we devise to use that common heritage must provide for the good of all and respect the rights of each. The measures adopted by new liberal governments to protect the rights of workers were measures aimed at protecting workers from the pressures of competition and from the bargaining power held by property owners. They aimed at guaranteeing that the advantages of private property would redound to the common good, and that private property would not undermine the liberty of individual workers. Such measures are fully consistent with strong rights of individual liberty and adventitious rights of private property. They are also consistent, or at least possibly consistent, with the utilitarian argument for private property. The libertarian argument against such measures presupposes a view of property rights that is not adequately supported by libertarian theory.

### The Role of Free Markets

In "What Libertarianism Is," John Hospers notes that many readers are apt to respond to libertarian proposals to eliminate all welfare safety nets with the rejoinder "But then you'd let people go hungry." Hospers continues:

> This, the libertarian insists, is precisely what would not happen; with the restrictions removed, the economy would flourish as never before. With the controls taken off business, existing enterprises would expand and new ones would spring into existence satisfying more and more consumer needs; millions more people would be gainfully employed instead of subsisting on welfare, and all kinds of research and production, released from the stranglehold of government, would proliferate, fulfilling man's needs and desires as never before. It has always been so whenever government has permitted men to be free traders on a free market.[22]

But has it always been so? Didn't laissez-faire capitalism export grain from Ireland while the Irish people starved? Didn't free markets gives us the sordid, dreary world described by Charles Dickens? Didn't capitalism drive the people of Britain off the land, forcing them to abandon farming beneath the open sky and leaving them prisoners in the darkness of the mines and factories? Didn't capitalism crush the bodies and spirits of whole generations of working men and women? Don't free markets bring the insecurity of periodic crises, with massive unemployment and attendant misery? Isn't Hospers's cheery optimism a testament to the power of ideology to ignore the facts?

Thinkers sympathetic to the libertarian outlook have tried to address the issues raised by these questions. In *Capitalism and the Historians,* F.A. Hayek edited a collection of essays devoted to showing that critics of capitalism had romanticized the past and that in fact, on the whole, the standard of living for the working class rose with the advent of capitalism and free trade in the nineteenth century.[23] Hayek also tried to show that the periodic depressions that seem to accompany the operations of free markets are really caused by misguided governmental interventions.[24] This idea was vindicated to some extent by Milton and Rose Friedman, who tried to show that the great depression of the 1930s was not the result of failures of the market, as has commonly been supposed, but rather the result of mistakes by those in charge of the Federal Reserve system in the United States.[25]

These and other studies of their kind are certainly important, but they fall far short of what is needed to sustain the libertarian position with respect to free markets. In the first place, the arguments of Hospers, Hayek, and the Friedmans sketched above all work within the framework of broadly utilitarian defenses of free markets. For the real libertarian, free markets must be preserved even if they have the disastrous consequences attributed to them by the romantic socialist. Beyond this, the arguments, which remain controversial, would not be adequate to support the view that no intervention in the operation of free markets is desirable even if they were true.

Suppose it is true that working-class wages were rising during the nineteenth century. Does it follow that new liberal measures that interfered with the operation of the market were misguided? Not at all. It is enough for the new liberal to argue that measures that interfered with the market could make things better. In an essay concerned with the problem of world hunger, the philosopher Peter Singer formulates a principle concerning avoidable suffering: "If it is in our power to prevent something bad from happening, without thereby sacrificing anything of comparable moral importance, we ought, morally to do it."[26] Now, even if it is true that living standards had improved under free-market capitalism, considerable poverty and suffering remained. What if, by interfering somewhat with the market, it was possible to reduce this remaining suffering without sacrificing anything of comparable moral importance? From the consequentialist point of view, to show this would be sufficient to justify market interference, and this is exactly the claim advanced by Hobhouse in making the case for new liberal measures: "The prime justification of this expenditure is that the prevention of suffering . . . [is a] duty to fulfil. Any common life based on avoidable suffering . . . is a life not of harmony but of discord."[27]

Of course, supporters of free markets are apt to argue that while Hobhouse and the new liberals may have thought they could do better than the free market, in fact they were mistaken, and the kinds of interferences with the market they initiated only ended up making things worse. This is the kind of argument favored by Hayek and the Friedmans, for example. But, in the end, this argument fails to convince.

If one looks at the whole historical record, from the dawn of free-market capitalism in the days of Adam Smith to the present, the evidence seems to support the new liberal position. While standards of living may have been rising under free-market capitalism, they did even better during the heyday of new liberal regulation, from 1945 to 1975. It is the welfare-state economies of Germany, Japan, and the Scandinavian countries that have, historically, provided the highest standards of living for the widest portion of people over the longest period of time. Further, to the extent that neoliberal policies have attempted to restore free markets in the period after 1975, they appear to have produced social polarization of the kind experienced in the early days of capitalism, with great wealth on one side matched by great poverty on the other. While this conclusion is based on a highly speculative reading of historical experience, an experience contaminated with all kinds of complexities, it seems closer to the mark of truth than the wild optimism of Hospers's own appeal to history.

Libertarianism offers a clear, coherent, and powerful conception of how societies ought to be organized. No doubt these are virtues in a theory. But, in the end, libertarianism illustrates the wisdom of Kant's point that a theory that doesn't work in practice is not good, even in theory.[28] In any case, Kant himself was no libertarian. He saw no contradiction between his prohibition against using people as mere means, and taxation for social welfare. He held that, "Indirectly, i.e. in so far as he takes the duty of the people upon himself, the supreme commander has the right to impose taxes upon the people for their own preservation, e.g. for the *care of the poor,* for *foundling hospitals* and *church activities,* or for what are otherwise known as charitable or pious institutions."[29]

# —— Chapter 9 ——
# A Deeper Sense of Politics

Traditionally, political philosophy has concerned itself with questions about the institutions of government and the relationship between government and the individual person. Is monarchy or democracy the better form of government? What are the limits of governmental power? These are examples of questions that are central to traditional political philosophy. They are questions that remain important for political philosophy and accordingly have been addressed in earlier chapters of this book. However, recent work in political philosophy has deepened our understanding of what is political. Traditional political philosophy has taken for granted a distinction between the public and the private. The public sphere is the sphere of government. The private sphere is the sphere of business, voluntary nongovernmental organizations, family, and individual life. Traditional political philosophy has concerned itself with the public sphere and with the proper boundary between the public and private. It has left the private sphere outside the scope of its concern. Recent political philosophy has challenged this limitation of the discipline's scope. It has called attention to the extent to which even the private sphere is shaped by philosophical assumptions, assumptions that assign specific roles to individual persons and that define these roles, at least in part, in terms of relationships of power and subordination that are highly political in nature. In earlier chapters we have already explored the extent to which the "private" sphere of business and economic life involves issues of justice that must be addressed by any adequate political philosophy. In this chapter we will explore how political ideas penetrate even deeper into the private realm, influencing our very conception of ourselves as individual human beings. As a way of getting at the kinds of issues involved, we will focus on matters of gender and race, but it should be noted that similar issues arise in considering, for example, how class, ethnicity, religion, and sexual orientation enter into our sense of who we are.

## The Political Philosophy of Patriarchy

As a way of getting at how political philosophy enters into the deepest recesses of the private sphere, let us consider briefly how philosophical ideas have shaped traditional ideas about women and the proper role of women in social life. For thousands of years, in Western societies at least, women have been assigned roles that make them subordinate to men. In the family, the church, the state, and all the important institutions of society, with some notable individual exceptions, men have held the positions of power. Women's rights have been restricted—often severely restricted. Women have been denied education, the right to own or control property, and the right to express their opinions or to participate in public life. They have been denied a say in how their children should be raised. They have even been denied control over their own bodies and their own sexual life. They have been controlled by the decisions of fathers, brothers, and husbands. Sometimes this control has been exercised with gentleness and respect; at other times it has been exercised with brutality and contempt.

This system of male domination, patriarchy, has been a central feature of human social existence for thousands of years. It has been so pervasive that until very recently most men and women have assumed that it reflected the natural order of things. But, in fact, this is not so. Patriarchy is a historical creation, made by human beings. Archaeological research points to the existence of societies in the Neolithic and the Bronze Age in which women played a more equal role. In much of the world early conceptions of God were of a female figure—a mother who gave birth to the natural universe and all living things and who continued to rule over it. Violent suppression of the religion of the mother God was a part of the historical process by which patriarchy came to be.[1]

While undoubtedly violence played a role in the creation of patriarchy, patriarchal institutions also received support from ways of thinking that depicted them as good, just, wise, divinely ordained, or natural. Religions were developed, Judaism, Christianity, and Islam among them, that centered around a father God and gave privileged positions to men. Art and literature told stories of the heroic actions of the mythic males who supposedly founded the ancient nations and gave them their laws. In these representations of history and social life, women were depicted as lesser beings, rightly assigned to subordinate and supporting roles. In this way, the belief that patriarchal institutions were good seeped into the thinking of women as well as men.

Western philosophy emerged after the establishment of patriarchal institutions. While some philosophers, such as Plato, questioned the view that women were rightly subordinate to men, it is not surprising that most philosophers were unable to escape the prevailing patriarchal prejudices that shaped the consciousness of their times.[2] Aristotle, who came after Plato, reaffirmed the superiority of males over females and defended slavery, arguing that some men were by nature masters and others by nature slaves.[3] Following Aristotle, almost all philosophers, these (male) lovers of wisdom, decided that male domination was natural and good. For two thousand years Western philosophers have been finding "reasons" to show that this was so.

Denied education, unable to read or write, most women had no opportunity to participate in the discussions of the philosophers. There were some exceptions. Hypatia, the daughter of a mathematician, was well educated in both mathematics and philosophy. She lectured on mathematics and philosophy in Alexandria, Egypt, becoming one of the world's leading geometers and heading the Neoplatonist school of philosophy there. Angered at her pagan religion and "the freedom of her ways," a mob, instigated by the Christian bishop of Alexandria, brutally murdered her in A.D. 415.[4] This suppression of the female voice has been with us for thousands of years. We can only speculate on what might have been said had women been given the opportunity to speak and write. In the absence of that voice, our collective consciousness of who women are, and what their role in society should be, has been largely shaped without the participation of women themselves.

It is only in the recent past that this has begun to change. The American and French Revolutions called into question age-old beliefs. They proclaimed the rights of men and advocated radical changes in the way society should be governed. In 1792 Mary Wollstonecraft published *A Vindication of the Rights of Women,* a work that applied the revolutionary philosophy of natural rights to the cause of emancipating women from the domination of men. It was not long before African-American slaves in the United States were appealing to the same revolutionary philosophy to demand their own emancipation. Though still incomplete, these struggles have initiated profound changes in our social existence and have forced a redefinition of the boundaries of political philosophy.

## Natural Rights and Human Nature

The theory of natural rights is embedded in the broader theory of natural law. According to that theory, the right way to use a thing was to use it in accordance with its nature. Aristotle took it as obvious that human beings differed in important ways in their natures. Of particular importance for Aristotle was whether or not human beings had a capacity for rational self-direction. Those men who had this capacity were rightly masters; those who lacked this capacity were rightly slaves. Aristotle thought of the having or not having of this capacity as a matter not of education or training but of nature: "From the hour of their birth, some are marked out for subjection, others for rule."[5] Of course there were some cases in which a man who had this capacity was enslaved, but in this case the man was being treated contrary to his nature and the enslavement was unjust. Similarly, there were cases where a man who lacked this capacity was in a position of mastery over others. This too, in Aristotle's view, was contrary to nature, and so unjust. However, where a man who had this capacity ruled over a man who lacked it, there was no injustice. Aristotle thought of women as having this capacity to some extent, but to a lesser extent than men, who were by nature masters. Thus, on Aristotle's view, in the well-ordered household, the husband ruled over his wife and over his slaves as well. In roughly this form, this view that men rightly should rule over women prevailed among almost all thinkers, including even such champions of the Enlightenment as Jean-Jacques Rousseau and Immanuel Kant.

Wollstonecraft's *A Vindication of the Rights of Women* directly challenged this way of thinking. Agreeing with the fundamental ideas of natural law and natural rights, she questioned the assumption that women lacked the power of rational self-direction, an assumption crucial to justification of the subordinate status of women and the denial of their equal rights:

> But if women are to be excluded, without having a voice, from a participation of the natural rights of mankind, prove first, to ward off the

charge of injustice and inconsistency, that they want reason, else this flaw in your NEW CONSTITUTION will ever show that man must, in some shape, act like a tyrant, and tyranny, in whatever part of society it rears its brazen front, will ever undermine morality.[6]

Wollstonecraft directly criticized the popular ideas of Rousseau, according to whom women were creatures of feeling rather than reason and according to whom "woman is made to please and to be dominated."[7] Like Aristotle and the other philosophers before him, Rousseau based his case regarding the proper role for women on observations of women around him. Admitting that many women were preoccupied with dress, appearance, and pleasing men, Wollstonecraft argued that this fact was a product of social conditioning rather than innate disposition. She also pointed out that this conditioning of women is but the obverse of a coin that includes the conditioning of men to lives of unreasoning brutishness. Throughout her book Wollstonecraft drives these points home, affirming the rational capacity of women, appealing to women to live up to their human nature, and appealing to men to cease oppressing women.

Wollstonecraft's opposition to the subordination of women to men worked within the framework of natural-law theory made popular, in some quarters at least, by the American and French Revolutions. Opposition to the enslavement of Africans in the Americas followed a similar pattern of argument. Although the enslavement of Africans by Europeans lacked the historical depth of the subordination of women to men, Europeans were quick to relegate Africans to Aristotle's category of natural slaves. Accordingly, the defense of slavery rested on the widely held assumption that Africans were inferior to Europeans, a view also endorsed by Kant and by the great Enlightenment naturalist Linnaeus, who classified Africans as the lowest of the four races of man and as properly to be "governed by the arbitrary will of his masters."[8] But like the view that women were incapable of rational self-direction, so too the view that Africans lacked this capacity was vulnerable to the refutation of experience. In his speech "What to the Slave Is the Fourth of July," delivered in 1852, when slavery was still widely accepted in the United States, Frederick Douglass effectively challenged this presupposition of African inferiority:

For the present, it is enough to affirm the equal manhood of the Negro race. Is it not astonishing that, while we are ploughing, planting, and

reaping, using all kinds of mechanical tools, erecting houses, construct-
ing bridges, building ships, working in metals of brass, iron, copper,
silver and gold; that, while we are reading, writing and ciphering, acting
as clerks, merchants and secretaries, having among us lawyers, doctors,
ministers, poets, authors, editors, orators and teachers; that, while we are
engaged in all manner of enterprises common to other men, digging gold
in California, capturing the whale in the Pacific, feeding sheep and cattle
on the hill-side, living, moving, acting, thinking, planning, living in families as husbands, wives and children, and above all, confessing and
worshipping the Christian's God, and looking hopefully for life and
immortality beyond the grave, we are called upon to prove that we are
men?[9]

Like Wollstonecraft, Douglass spoke on behalf of an "other" ban-
ished from the family of humankind by the prejudices of the dominant
group of males of northern European descent. And, like Wollstonecraft, by the very eloquence and power of his argument, he undermined the justification of that banishment.

Sadly, discrimination against women and African-Americans continued long after the arguments of Wollstonecraft and Douglass had
been heard. Indeed, in the late nineteenth and early twentieth centuries,
views that women and Africans were inferior to European males in
their capacity for rational self-direction were reinforced by the pronouncements of modern "science."

Having won legal equality in the early twentieth century, by mid-
century women faced the hostile pronouncements of Freudian psychology, according to which a woman's interest in work outside the home was
viewed as a sign of an unsuccessful navigation of the path to normal adult
development.[10] Although now widely viewed as pseudoscience, Freud's
theory haunted the lives of a whole generation of women, relegating them
to the traditional roles of mother and supportive wife.

African-Americans also faced a scientific establishment that pro-
nounced them inferior to whites. By the turn of the century, theories
that classified humankind into a variety of different races and ranked
them as higher or lower in terms of intellectual and moral capacities
were widely accepted by both the intellectual establishment and popular consciousness in northern Europe and North America. Not surprisingly, these theories placed people of northern European extraction at
the top of the hierarchy of races and, reflecting the racist heritage of
the era of the slave trade, put people of African extraction at the

bottom of the hierarchy. Though the theories were irredeemably flawed pseudoscience, they were widely accepted and had a significant influence on both public consciousness and public policy.[11] Like women, African-Americans faced a long struggle before their equal humanity came to be acknowledged, a struggle fought as much on the terrain of science as on the terrain of ethics. By now the natural equality of all human beings is widely, though not universally, accepted. Still, important differences remain about how current public policy should reflect this equality.

## Formal and Fair Equality of Opportunity

Before the Civil War, the laws of the United States and the laws of the various states discriminated against women and African-Americans. Neither was permitted to vote or to hold office, for example. Formal equality of opportunity involves doing away with such explicit legal discrimination. Formal equality is also often understood to involve the elimination of discriminatory private rules and practices that, while they lack the status of law, nonetheless function to explicitly exclude people of certain categories from certain opportunities. For example, in the nineteenth century many universities, law schools, and medical schools explicitly denied admission to women. Formal equality of opportunity involves the elimination of all such explicitly discriminatory rules, laws, and regulations. In the United States, despite some notable exceptions in private educational institutions and social clubs, women had largely won formal equality of opportunity by the 1920s.

African-Americans were less fortunate. Despite some gains in the direction of formal equality in the Thirteenth, Fourteenth, and Fifteenth Amendments to the Constitution, the Compromise of 1876 allowed the states to reestablish extensive systems of legal discrimination. These "Jim Crow" laws remained in effect until finally overcome by the civil rights movement in the 1960s.

While formal equality was a major step forward for women and for African-Americans, significant disadvantages remained. A medical school may drop its explicit rule against admitting black students, but without an education, the formal right to be considered equally with white applicants from privileged backgrounds is an empty one. Fair equality of opportunity involves, in addition to formal equality, the social guarantee of the resources necessary to make formal equality more than an empty right. It is fair equality of opportunity that is required by Rawls's principles of justice. In the United States, the commitment to fair equality of opportunity has been most significantly expressed in the commitment to public education, to the provision of the educational resources necessary for fair as opposed to merely formal equality of opportunity. In fact, however, there are rather severe limits to the achievement of fair equality of opportunity. In the United States, funding for public schools remains based largely on property taxes. The effect of this is to give far more educational resources to students from wealthy suburbs than is available to students from poorer inner-city and rural areas. Children from wealthier homes are also apt to have available opportunities for private lessons in music, sports, and the arts, and to have opportunities for travel, opportunities that better prepare the child to compete for positions. In addition to these limits to fair opportunity, there are also limits of a different kind, limits that have been addressed by policies of affirmative action. In the next section we will examine the idea of affirmative action and some of the issues connected with that idea.

**Affirmative Action**

Let us suppose a society in which formal and fair equality of opportunity have been achieved. There are no rules or laws banning groups from certain positions, and individuals in all groups have access to sufficient resources to allow them to compete for positions. Suppose, however, that there remain widespread prejudices that stigmatize members of a certain group as intellectually or morally inferior. Being subject to these prejudices, admissions officers and prospective employers are going to be apt to pass over applications from members of the stigmatized group. They are also apt to feel less comfortable, more suspicious, and more critical while interviewing members of the stigmatized group. For these reasons, given a choice between two more or less equally qualified applicants, decision makers are apt to prefer the individual they are comfortable with over the individual from the stigmatized group. Given the widespread nature of the prejudice against members of the group, even with formal and fair equality of opportunity, members of the group are likely to be systematically excluded from attractive and rewarding positions in the social structure.

Though fair equality of opportunity was also missing in the period just after the final demise of formal discrimination against them, African-Americans in the United States faced widespread prejudices of just this kind. To a certain extent, women too found themselves in such a situation. It was not at all uncommon in the late 1960s for women applicants to medical school or law school to be passed over for financial aid because administrators believed they would marry and drop out of school, thereby wasting the aid that was given them. It was also not at all uncommon for a woman or African-American to be passed over because the prejudices of the relevant decision maker were so strong that he could not accept an apparent equality of credentials as real.

Affirmative action aimed at rectifying the injustices persisting because of such prejudices. A series of federal and state mandates were issued requiring institutions receiving government money to take affirmative steps to find, recruit, hire, or appoint qualified applicants from groups that were victims of prejudices that worked to unfairly exclude them. Proponents of affirmative action justified such measures on two grounds: that it was just restitution to victims of past wrongdoing, and that it would produce a better society in the future, a society that was both happier and more just.

From the beginning, affirmative action was sharply criticized. For restitution to be just, it was said, it needs to compensate the actual victims of wrongdoing. But affirmative action awarded benefits to individuals who may not themselves have been victims of wrongdoing. Further, critics argued, women and racial minorities are not the only victims of past wrongdoing. The Irish, for example, were victimized by prejudice and discrimination for several generations. In selecting women and racial minorities for current restitution, affirmative action unfairly privileges some victims over others. Critics also argued that affirmative action constitutes "reverse discrimination," substituting discrimination against white males for discrimination against women and racial minorities, thereby creating more victims of wrongdoing. Justice, the critics held, requires that positions go to those most qualified to fill them. It was wrong to consider gender or race in the past, and it is wrong to consider them now.

Defenders of affirmative action replied that we commonly provide restitution to the descendants of those who have been wronged, as, for example, when we require that property belonging to Jews who perished in the Holocaust be returned to their descendants or to other victims of the Holocaust when no such descendants can be found. They also argued that while other groups and other individuals did suffer discrimination, racial minorities and women have suffered more persistent and damaging discrimination, and that, in any case, more justice is better than less even if it is not perfect.

Defenders of affirmative action also pointed out that it is questionable whether justice requires that positions go solely to those most qualified for them. We have long accepted consideration of geographic distribution as one criterion for admission to educational institutions. Why is consideration of racial distribution an injustice if consideration of geography is not? In any case, defenders of affirmative action have argued that we need to do something to create a happier and more just society in the future. Affirmative action is necessary to achieve this end.

Opponents of affirmative action have argued that the future-regarding case for affirmative action is just as weak as the case based on restitution for past wrongdoing. It is to the good of society as a whole if positions are filled by those best qualified to hold them. Each of us want the best doctor and the best mechanic. In making race and gender count, affirmative action undermines the principle of merit, which best serves the interests of society as a whole. Further, critics of affirmative action argue, affirmative action actually ends up reinforcing prejudices and injuring the very people it seeks to help. The black person who does happen to be the best-qualified person for a job will be widely viewed as having gotten the position not because of qualifications but because of race. To this skepticism and distrust of blacks in positions of importance will be added a dose of resentment from white males who will feel that they have been unfairly overlooked. In such a climate, racial prejudices are likely to deepen, not subside. The only correct policy, the critics argue, is a color-blind policy that does not consider race or gender at all.

Defenders of affirmative action reply that race and gender should count only in selecting from among qualified applicants. Further, they argue, while the public may face black holders of positions with some degree of skepticism and distrust, experience in dealing with the many qualified blacks who do come to hold positions will erode that skepticism and distrust, experience that the majority population would likely never have without some form of affirmative action. Finally, supporters of affirmative action are likely to point out that the "color-blind" policy recommended by opponents of affirmative action is a fantasy. In the United States at least, color consciousness and prejudice based on color consciousness are too deeply ingrained to make any truly color-blind decision making possible. It is an indication of the depth of the problem, and something of a grotesque irony as well, that Charles Murray, who has publicly argued for color-blind repeal of affirmative action policies on the ground that the old racial prejudices have been largely overcome, is himself coauthor of a book purporting to show that blacks are genetically determined to have lower IQs than whites, a book that made the best-seller lists in the United States.[12] It is surely unrealistic to think that a society in which such a book makes the best-seller list is a society that can ignore race.

## The Personal and the Political

Traditionally, political philosophy has focused on the institutions of government and their relationship to individual citizens. But thinking about the role of women and racial minorities in the history of the United States has led us to see how aspects of our lives, such as gender and race, that we tend to think of as personal and outside the realm of concern of political philosophy are in fact highly politicized. These politicized conceptions of gender and race are reflected in the roles traditionally assigned to particular individuals. Affirmative action policies try to subvert these politicized roles by opening doors for qualified individuals from traditionally oppressed groups to enter desirable positions. But such efforts cannot address the full range of constraints affecting the lives of people from such groups.

Consider, for example, the "personal" difficulties facing women today. Though most women have sometimes worked outside the home, and many women have worked a great deal outside the home, the traditional woman's role has required a substantial amount of domestic labor and primary responsibility for child care. With these demands upon their time, many women have found it necessary to forgo career opportunities outside the home, even when such opportunities arise. Consequently, women are dependent upon their husbands for the income necessary to sustain the home. But this dependence brings with it a certain degree of risk. Being dependent upon her husband for the support of herself and her children, the wife is vulnerable to spousal abuse. Such abuse, whether physical or psychological, has, unhappily, been far from uncommon. In a famous letter to her husband, John

Adams, written just a few months before the signing of the Declaration of Independence, Abigail Adams makes reference to the abuses suffered by women at the hands of men:

> That your Sex are Naturally Tyrannical is a Truth so thoroughly established as to admit of no dispute, but such of you as wish to be happy willingly give up the harsh title of Master for the more tender and endearing one of Friend. Why then, not put it out of the power of the vicious and the Lawless to use us with cruelty and indignity with impunity? Men of Sense in all Ages abhor those customs which treat us only as the vassals of your Sex.[13]

What this letter clearly reveals is a hidden political dimension to the relations between husband and wife. Custom gave to men power over their wives. What Abigail Adams sought was political action that would limit men's power. Sadly, though he was undoubtedly among those men who aspire to be friends rather than masters, John Adams was unwilling to interfere in these matters, leaving in place those ancient customs that left women subject to the cruelties and indignities of their husbands. It is only now, under the impetus of modern feminism, that some efforts are being made to address these issues. But even now, with laws against spousal abuse, and with shelters for battered women, her condition of economic dependence makes it difficult for a woman to escape an abusive husband. What will she do? If she takes a job, what will become of her children? Affordable child care is simply not available for all who need it.

The state of dependency forced upon a woman by the responsibilities of home and children also makes her vulnerable to economic ruin. In California, men increase their standard of living by 42 percent following divorce, while women's standard of living declines by 73 percent.[14] Women are faced with a choice: between marriage and children, on one hand, and an upwardly mobile career path, on the other. In agreeing to marriage, and in taking on the responsibilities of home and child care, women are forced to give less time to their careers. Consequently, their earning power, even if they eventually return to full-time work, is likely to be far less than that of a man who made a primary commitment to his career. Having made the commitment to marriage, the woman now finds herself in desperate economic straits when the marriage collapses. Now, where formal and fair equality of opportunity obtain, it is possible for a woman to avoid economic dependency provided she is willing to give up home and family or provided she is lucky enough to find a man willing to run the risks traditionally run by women. But for the vast majority of women, home and family life remain highly valuable, and the vast majority of women end up with the primary responsibility for home and children. The problem of dependence and its risks remains a serious matter for very many women.

These aspects of the choices faced by women are by now commonplace. The feminization of poverty has become well known. The point here is just that these now-familiar facts highlight some very difficult problems that have not been addressed by traditional political theory. Formal equality, fair equality, and affirmative action, even if perfectly applied, would not suffice to liberate women so long as women carry their traditional responsibilities. How can we reconcile the needs of home and children with free-market economics and free-market labor markets? What business can remain competitive when it alone allows a woman to take substantial time off from her job? What business can remain competitive when it alone offers good-paying jobs to women whose skills have been eroded by years away from their profession?

Perhaps even deeper than this is the simple matter of the direct relationship between the sexes. Men and women alike carry in their heads prejudices that tend to value men's lives more than women's lives. These prejudices are relics of past ideologies, of the ideas of Aristotle and the other philosophers who relegated women to subordinate roles. In this sense, political philosophy enters not just into the framework of the institutions we inhabit, but into the soul itself. Despite all of the attention that the effects of advertising, pornography, and the acculturation of children have received, it remains true that many men and women continue to see women in much the same way as women were seen in the days of Mary Wollstonecraft, as ornaments, playthings, and servants of men. At its most basic level, perhaps, the problem is that because women and men alike are deluded by false conceptions of women, women are not treated with the respect due them as human beings. From this point of view, one of the central tasks of political philosophy must be to bring this false consciousness to light. But there remains also another task as well: that of trying to conceive how society could be remade so as to free women from the difficult choices and traps forced upon them by the weight of tradition and the way society is now organized. The true liberation of women will require both a change in the consciousness of human beings and a change in the social structures within which we live our lives.

## Emancipatory Consciousness

In *The Wretched of the Earth,* the psychologist Frantz Fanon describes the destructive consequences of racism on the lives of Algerians before the time of Algerian independence.[15] Fanon emphasizes the extent to which racism poisons the consciousness of those who are stigmatized by it. Racism is internalized. It turns a people against themselves. Violence against one's own people, suicide, destructive patterns of behavior, derision of oneself and others—these are all symptoms of internalized racism. Like the idea that women are rightly subordinate to men, racist ideas enter into the consciousness of individuals on both sides of racial divides, sustaining illusions of superiority and inferiority and undermining the sense of mutual respect necessary for just relationships. Just as political philosophy must bring to light and expose the illusions of sexism, so too it must bring to light and expose the illusions of racism.

This conception of philosophy as devoted to criticizing false consciousness and thereby making possible the emancipation of human beings from the oppressive social relationships sustained by that false consciousness is known as critical theory. It is a view of philosophy that reaches back to the middle of the nineteenth century and finds its exemplar in the work of Karl Marx. Marx conceived of his task as a critique of political economy. He aimed at unmasking the claims of his contemporaries that the laws of the market were, like the laws of chemistry, natural and consequently unavoidable. Marx labored to show that free-market capitalism was the historical product of human making and therefore subject to revision or replacement by other forms of life. In the same way, contemporary feminist philosophers and philosophers concerned with race seek to find the hidden assumptions that enter into our sense of who we are and what are our relationships with others, and to expose these assumptions to the light of critical examination, aiming thereby at the emancipation of those who are oppressed by relationships and institutions based upon such assumptions.[16]

The German philosopher Jürgen Habermas is an important current representative of critical theory. While many feminist and African-American philosophers would not consider themselves Habermasians, nonetheless, Habermas's ideas have had a strong influence on feminist philosophy and upon philosophies of liberation in all parts of the world. While Habermas's philosophy is complex and difficult, we can get a sense of some of his basic ideas by seeing how the framework he developed can be applied to problems of racial and sexual oppression.

When I make any kind of claim in philosophy, my making that claim carries with it an implicit commitment to reason. If I say that members of one group should be treated differently than members of another group, I open myself up to the question as to why this should be so. But the reason that I offer is itself open to further questioning; for example, Wollstonecraft and Douglass questioned the reasons offered in support of discrimination against women and Africans. Habermas conceives of philosophy as an open-ended dialogue in which every statement carries with it an implicit commitment to reply to any and all questions that might be raised by serious and fair interlocutors. Attempts to exclude questions or persons, or attempts to close the dialogue before all questions and views have been heard, involve arbitrary interventions that violate the commitment to reason implicit in the very first attempt to say something about the world. Such arbitrary interventions are, in this sense, a betrayal of reason, and it is one of the tasks of philosophy to protest against such betrayals. For Habermas, the correct answer is the one that would emerge at the end of such an open-ended dialogue where every individual is given the opportunity to speak and question until no further questions remain. Of course, no actual dialogue can satisfy this ideal, but the ideal provides the basis for a critique of actual political discourse. Habermas's work draws our attention to the moral and political significance of excluded voices, the voices of women, of racial, religious, and ethnic minorities, of homosexuals, and of the poor. Unlike natural-law theory and utilitarianism, which are essentially "monological," deriving claims about the rightness of certain political and social arrangements by logical inference from abstract principles, Habermas's approach rests on "dialogical" foundations, which require the genuine participation of these excluded voices. While there is considerable theoretical controversy about Habermas's claim that commitment to certain moral principles is inherent in the use of language, Habermas's framework provides a model for understanding much of the work that philosophers have done in critically examining racial and sexual oppression.[17]

There are, however, a number of philosophers who feel that an adequate philosophical understanding of emancipatory consciousness forces us to step outside the boundaries of critical theory as it was understood by Marx and is understood by Habermas. These philosophers believe that a philosophically adequate understanding of emancipatory consciousness must incorporate some of the ideas of the poststructuralist or postmodernist philosophies developed by Michel Foucault, Jacques Derrida, Gilles Deleuze, Julia Kristeva, Luce Irigaray, and a number of other French thinkers in the 1970s and 1980s. While we cannot do justice to any of these thinkers here and while important difference exist between them, nevertheless we can sketch some ideas that have emerged from this body of work that some philosophers have found important for understanding emancipatory consciousness.

Like the critical theorists, the postmodernists emphasize that our consciousness of ourselves, other people, and the world around us is a historically constructed system of ideas. Like the critical theorists, the postmodernists view us as, so to speak, prisoners of these constructed ideologies. Thus, for example, women grow up thinking of themselves as inferior or subordinate to men because they internalize the historically constructed ideology of patriarchy. Critical theory aims at dispelling the power of this ideology by showing that it is false. But to show that something is false, it is necessary to shine the light of truth upon it. In this respect, critical theory might be said to agree with the biblical idea that knowledge of the truth will set us free.[18] But this, the postmodernists say, is to assume a dichotomy of truth and falsehood that cannot itself withstand critical reflection.

According to the postmodernists, it is not only the systems of beliefs about the world and our place in it but also our methods of reasoning and standards of evaluation that are historically constructed. We believe that there are "true" and "false" representations of the world, and that there are standards of logic and good reasoning that will allow us to discern which is which. But in fact, the postmodernist argues, all we humans can ever reach with our thought is our own constructed image. Insofar as the world is for us at all, it is as an image constructed by our own consciousness of it. Further, the postmodernist argues, this image-making thought that is for us inescapable is always historically situated. It is the thought of a man or a woman, a European or an African, a worker or a capitalist. The critical theorist is in a sense insufficiently critical, forgetting that the subject of thought and the very canons of rationality that that subject embraces are in reality parts of a complex, particular, constructed subjectivity.

The postmodernist says that despite its talk of dialogue, critical theory imagines that all of us share some purely logical consciousness, unsullied by prejudices growing out of a particular situation in life. Critical theory addresses itself to this pure consciousness, a consciousness that, because it has been purified of all particularity and all prejudice, is universal, standing for the consciousness of each and every one of us. It is this pure consciousness that makes possible the kind of dialogue imagined by the critical theorist, a dialogue that reaches some agreement. But, not surprisingly, being themselves not pure consciousness but particular, embodied, and usually male consciousnesses, critical theorists mistake their own masculine, white, European, bourgeois consciousness for the universal consciousness of everyone engaged in the dialogue. Behind the emancipatory mask of critical theory stands the prison of a particular way of thought passing itself off for the one, true, universally valid way of thought.

Guarding against this error, postmodernist understandings of emancipatory consciousness stress the importance of recognizing the validity of the consciousness of particular women and particular people of color. They resist attempts to validate one voice and discredit another, arguing that any such judgments rest on unsustainable claims to universality and objectivity. But beyond this they also reject the assumption underlying critical theory that there is some universal logic guaranteeing that different points of view can, eventually, come to agreement about what is right and true. For the postmodernist, genuine respect for others must rest content with the irredeemable otherness of others and the existence of multiple "truths"; the tyranny of objective truth must give way to the tolerance of subjective opinion.[19]

Though on the surface well suited to support the expression of views by oppressed and marginalized peoples, in the end the postmodernist perspective seems untenable. While it is undoubtedly true that prejudices often have paraded behind the mask of objective truth, the very unmasking of such claims seems to presuppose the possibility of valid judgments between conflicting truth claims.

Consider, for example, the struggle to overcome legal discrimination against women and African-Americans. In the early years of the American republic, it was thought that there were important differences, with respect to the capacity for rational self-direction, between males of northern European descent and males of African descent, as well as important differences in this same respect between males and females. But whether or not Africans or women have this capacity is a question of fact, at least to a significant degree. Scientific racism claimed to provide factual evidence to support its conclusions about Africans. But this evidence did not stand up. Nor did the widely accepted view that women were incapable of rationally governing their own lives stand up to the critical challenge raised by Wollstonecraft and others. When the evidence points against the belief necessary to justify discriminatory practices, those discriminatory practices become difficult to defend. This point shows the inadequacy of the view that political commitments are subjective, that in politics there are only opinions and that no opinion is better than any other. In fact, political commitments are entangled with questions of fact, questions that are at least in principle answerable. In its criticism of objectivity and the canons of scientific rationality as themselves merely subjective points of view, postmodernist philosophy appears to be mistaken. Our brief examination of the real histories of debates over gender and race seems to show not a confrontation between incommensurable standpoints but a dialogue between "others" who, despite their differences, can communicate with one another and work toward a shared resolution of their differences.

## Structures

Political ideas enter into our sense of who we are and what our relationships with other people should be. In this chapter we have focused on how such political ideas have functioned to sustain sexism and racism and how philosophy can attempt to emancipate women and individuals belonging to racial minorities from the oppressive power of those ideas. But, as we saw in considering the real structural constraints imposed on women by the conflicting claims of career and family, emancipation cannot be entirely a matter of consciousness raising. Emancipation may require, as well, changes in the institutional structures of the society within which we live. In the next chapter we will examine some such institutional structures. In particular, we will focus on how global markets provide an institutional structure that shapes the world we inhabit. We will examine some issues relevant to political philosophy that arise out of the way this structure works. If in this chapter we have examined how politics penetrates our very soul, in the next chapter we will examine how politics is present in our relationship with faraway places and peoples.

—— Chapter 10 ——

# Global Politics

Traditionally, political philosophy has speculated about what the institutions of the ideal state would be like. Although there has been some concern with relations between states, as for example in theories of just and unjust wars, for the most part attention has been focused on the institutions of the single state and the relationship between those institutions and the individual citizens of that state. However, as we come to the end of the twentieth century and the beginning of a new millennium, nation-states find themselves increasingly bound up in institutions, processes, and events that are international in scope. There is, as former U.S. president George Bush said, an emerging new world order. Any political philosophy adequate for our times must consider this new world order. It is the task of this chapter to contribute to this consideration.

In particular, we will focus on some issues raised by the role of global markets in shaping the international order. At this point in time the global market functions as the primary institution integrating the separate nation-states and separate peoples of the world into one international order. Political institutions such as the United Nations do certainly play a role, but, at least at this point in time, these institutions are weak, having little power to control events. The global market, on the other hand, already appears sufficiently powerful to threaten the very sovereignty of nation-states. It serves as the dominant institution of the new world order. It provides the structure within which every nation and every individual must live. In this chapter we will consider some issues raised by the structure the global market imposes on the emerging international order.

**Imperialism**

In the last chapter we looked at racism, with a focus on African Americans and racial minorities within the United States. But racism, of course, is not confined to the borders of the United States. The hierarchy of the races established by the pseudoscientific theories of race popular in the late nineteenth and early twentieth centuries cast a shadow that covered the entire globe. Those racial theories provided the supposed moral justification for European and North American imperialism, which in the late nineteenth and early twentieth centuries carved up the globe, assigning each part of it to the dominion of one of the imperial powers. The relatively brief period of imperial domination established the institutional foundation upon which the present is built, and it inflicted wounds on the colonized peoples of the world that have not yet healed. Any adequate political philosophy must address a range of current issues rooted in the experience of imperialism. Writing in the early hours of this century, W.E.B. DuBois clearly stated the problem. "The problem of the twentieth century," he said, "is the problem of the color-line,—the relation of the darker to the lighter races of men in Asia and Africa, in America and the islands of the sea."[1]

Classic colonialism took the form of direct political control of the colonized region, though that control often employed a bureaucracy and police force made up, at least at the lower levels, of indigenous peoples. Such direct political control, involving if necessary the coercive use of the military forces of the imperial power, clashed with at least some versions of natural-law theory. In proclaiming the decision of the people of the American colonies to become independent of Great Britain, the American Declaration of Independence refers to "the separate and equal station to which the Laws of Nature and of Nature's God entitle them." Such a right to self-determination seems flatly inconsistent with colonialism. If a people has a natural right to a separate and equal station among the nations of the world, then no foreign power may rightly rule over them, at least not without their consent. Taking the brave words of the American Declaration of Independence as their philosophical creed, and the anticolonial struggle of the American Revolution as their model, colonized people around the world struggled to gain national independence from their colonial rulers.[2] One by one the colonized regions of the world gained their independence, becoming equals among the sovereign powers of the world.

The right to self-determination claimed by the Americans and by other anticolonialists is not without its difficulties. In the first place, despite the words of the American Declaration, it is hard to see how such a right could be a natural right, like the rights to liberty and life. The right to liberty and the right to life belong to individual human beings, beings that are natural objects. Nations, on the other hand, are very different kinds of things. They are collections of people. But collections are, in a sense, not natural. They are products of human history and human making. How can such artificial entities have natural rights?

It might seem that this difficulty could be circumvented by making the national right to self-determination a right derived from the individual right of liberty possessed by each individual. If each individual Filipino desires freedom from American colonial rule, then for the United States to maintain that rule is for it to violate the right of liberty of the various individual people who constitute the Filipino nation. But this line of thinking seems to have dangerous implications. If I and three of my friends decide to form an independent country, do we have a natural right to do so?

Typically, at least, the right to self-determination is construed as a collective right distinct from the right to liberty of individual human beings. Julius Nyerere, for example, identifies three basic kinds of rights: the national right of self-determination, the individual right to liberty, and an individual right to freedom from hunger, poverty, and disease.[3] Here the right to self-determination attaches itself to a nation constituted by the shared history and traditions of a group of people. This leaves us then with the problem of how such a historically constituted entity can have a natural right. There are also problems about what distinguishes a group having the right to self-determination from a group that lacks that right. Do all people having a shared history and tradition constitute a nation? Do all such nations have a right to form independent sovereign states? In the American Civil War, Southerners claimed distinct nationhood on the basis of shared history and traditions. Did the Southern states then have a right to secede from the union? Do the Bosnian Serbs, who undeniably have a shared history and shared traditions, have a right to self-determination? There seems to be no theoretically satisfactory way to answer these questions.

In any case, in the aftermath of World War II, the formerly colonized nations of the world claimed their independence. But the independence they gained was only formal. In many ways, and to greater or lesser degrees, these newly independent nations remained under the control of their former colonizers. In some cases the former imperial powers maintained control through puppet regimes that, though they claimed to represent the peoples of the new nation, in fact served the interests of the former colonial power. In other cases the institutions created in the colonial era made it difficult or impossible for the newly independent country to control its fate. Of particular importance in this regard is the role of international markets. During the colonial era, vast regions of Asia and Africa were integrated into the structure of global capitalism. Most often, the colonies served as sources of raw materials and as markets for manufactured goods. With the end of direct colonial rule, newly independent governments found their options severely limited by the constraints imposed upon them by their nation's role in the global capitalist system. The locus of control had shifted from foreign governments to foreign banks, but control remained outside the formally independent nation. Classical colonialism, involving the direct control of external political power, had come to be replaced by neocolonialism, involving the indirect control of the world market and the financial institutions of the developed capitalist world, such as the World Bank and the International Monetary Fund. Capitalism had become a world system marked by a division between developed and underdeveloped countries, with the formerly colonized regions of the world falling among the underdeveloped countries.

In the decades after World War II, as the division between developed and underdeveloped parts of the world became clear, there was a revival of interest in Marxist theories of imperialism. While Marx's own scientific work focused on the theory of capitalism as a self-contained and isolated system, the generation of Marxists who came after Marx attempted to extend the Marxist theory of capitalism to include the interaction between capitalist economies and precapitalist economies that occurred in the era of imperialism. Incorporating the theory of imperialism developed by J.A. Hobson, who was not a Marxist, the Marxist thinkers Rudolf Hilferding, Rosa Luxemburg, Nikolai Bukharin, and V.I. Lenin attempted to work out an understanding of imperialism as the necessary outcome of capitalism. Despite important differences, these thinkers all agreed in seeing imperialism as a safety valve for capitalism. According to Marxist theory, as capitalism developed, it encountered increasingly deep and frequent crises, resulting in business failures, deep cuts in production, and unemployment. Expansion overseas relieved some of this pressure by providing new markets for the glut of products produced and by providing higher returns on investment. Nonetheless, according to these classical Marxist theories, capitalism contained within it a system of incentives that would lead to increasingly rapid development. This being so, the export of capitalism to other parts of the world should eventually result in the development of those other parts of the world. From the viewpoint of classical Marxism, one would expect that eventually the entire world would be more or less evenly developed into a single capitalist system of the kind analyzed by Marx.

By the 1960s and 1970s, with the division between developed and undeveloped parts of the world appearing largely unchanged since World War II, new "structural" theories of imperialism appeared. André Gunder Frank and Immanuel Wallerstein developed an account of the world capitalist system that saw the appearance of a developed center and a permanently underdeveloped periphery as inevitable structural features of capitalist economies. In this respect their theories broke radically with the traditional view that capitalism would inevitably lead to universal development. But Frank and Wallerstein retained a link with classical Marxism in their idea of the importance of exploitation as a feature of capitalism. According to their theories, exploitation of the underdeveloped periphery by the developed center was also a necessary feature of the world capitalist system. On this view, so long as the former colonies remained dependent upon the world capitalist system, they would be locked into underdevelopment, with all of the surplus wealth necessary for development being exported to the centers of the system. Indeed, according to these structural theories, the pattern of "underdevelopment" found in countries on the periphery of world capitalism was not simply an extension of a precapitalist past, but rather something produced by capitalism. Accordingly, development could come only by breaking with the world capitalist system, a conclusion that was also reached by Samir Amin in his refinements of the theory and by the independent account of imperialism, stressing unequal terms of trade within the world capitalist system, developed by Arghiri Emmanuel.

Despite their significant contributions to understanding capitalism as a world system, because of internal difficulties and because of evidence of development in some of the underdeveloped parts of the world, none of these theories appears to be ultimately successful.[4] The view that capitalism necessarily produces a developed center accompanied by an underdeveloped periphery has given way to the view that eventually capitalism will produce a more or less uniform worldwide state of development, with classical Marxists and champions of free-market capitalism agreeing in blaming the protracted phenomenon of underdevelopment on mistakes made within the former colonized regions of the world.

Nonetheless, enormous disparities exist between the standard of living that prevails in developed countries and that in the underdeveloped parts of the world, a division that often coincides with the color line pointed out by DuBois. In much of the underdeveloped world life is hard and short. Must we fold our hands and tell the poor of the world that eventually things will get better? Have we an obligation to provide them aid?

**Lifeboat Ethics**

In the 1970s, with episodes of widespread starvation breaking out in different parts of the world, proposals were made to establish a world food bank that would store supplies of grain for distribution when emergency situations produced the need for it. In a much-discussed article Garrett Hardin, a professor of biology and student of population growth, argued against this proposal. He compared the nations of the world to lifeboats and the plight of starving people to the plight of people who had fallen overboard.

> Approximately two-thirds of the world is desperately poor, and only one-third is comparatively rich. The people in poor countries have an average per capital GNP (Gross National Product) of about $200 per year; the rich, of about $3,000. (For the United States it is nearly $5,000 per year.) Metaphorically, each rich nation amounts to a lifeboat full of comparatively rich people. The poor of the world are in other, much more crowded lifeboats. Continuously, so to speak, the poor fall out of their lifeboats and swim for a while in the water outside, hoping to be admitted to a rich lifeboat, or in some other way to benefit from the "goodies" on board. What should the passengers on a rich lifeboat do? This is the central problem of "the ethics of a lifeboat."[5]

No doubt each of us feels sympathy for the plight of those who are about to drown. Our natural impulse would be to pull from the sea into our lifeboat as many as we possibly could. But of course, each lifeboat has a limited carrying capacity. If we give free rein to our feelings of sympathy, we will pull too many people aboard, the lifeboat will be swamped, and we will all drown. Difficult as it may be, we must hold our sympathy in check.

But what does this lifeboat ethics have to do with aid to starving people? An important element in Hardin's argument has to do with what he calls "the tragedy of the commons."

> The fundamental error of the sharing ethics is that it leads to the tragedy of the commons. Under a system of private property the man (or group of men) who own property recognize their responsibility to care for it, for if they don't they will eventually suffer. A farmer, for instance, if he is intelligent, will allow no more cattle in a pasture than its carrying capacity justifies. If he overloads the pasture, weeds take over, erosion sets in, and the owner loses in the long run. But if a pasture is run as a commons open to all, the right of each to use it is not matched by an operational responsibility to take care of it. It is no use asking independent herdsmen in a commons to act responsibly, for they dare not. The considerate herdsman who refrains from overloading the commons suffers more than a selfish one who says his needs are greater. (As Leo Durocher says, "Nice guys finish last.") Christian-Marxian idealism is counterproductive.[6]

Hardin argues that a world food bank would function like a common pasture. Its resources would be open to all who want to use them, with no corresponding responsibility for protecting the resource. But this undermines any incentive to behave in a responsible way. In particular, Hardin thinks the existence of a world food bank would undermine incentives for underdeveloped countries to control human birth rates. Requiring each country to feed its own people forces each country to protect the resources necessary to grow or purchase food and forces each country to limit its population to what it can afford to feed. If a country could turn to a world food bank whenever the needs of its population outstripped its own resources, its already too large population would be fed, would reproduce, and would create even greater demands upon the world food bank in future years. Eventually such unchecked population growth would produce a demand not even the world food bank could meet. Like the overloaded lifeboat, planet earth would be swamped by a population that exceeds its carrying capacity. Hardin concludes that rich countries should give food aid to poor countries only in emergency situations, and only then if the poor country has acted responsibly to husband its resources and limit its population.

Hardin's argument has been criticized because of the many morally relevant features of the real world omitted by his metaphor of the lifeboat. Why do some people, overwhelmingly people of color from Asia and Africa, just happen to find themselves in overcrowded lifeboats? According to at least one authority, Bangladesh, among the poorest and most overcrowded of "lifeboats," once had a prosperous economy, an economy that was reduced to poverty by British imperialism.[7] To the extent that current patterns of development and underdevelopment were produced by the actions of the imperial powers, surely those powers have some duties of restitution. Hardin ignores this history, taking the overcrowding in some lifeboats for granted.

Also missing from Hardin's analogy is any characterization of the amount of room occupied by the rich who luckily find themselves in one of the less crowded lifeboats. The average American uses up to thirty times as much of the earth's resources as the average Asian or African.[8] Hardin focuses on birth rates in the underdeveloped world, which undoubtedly do increase pressure on world resources, but ignores consumption rates in the developed world, which put much greater per capita stress on the carrying capacity of the planet.

Related to this point is another facet of the real world obscured by Hardin's argument. Guatemala is one of those countries Hardin would describe as an overcrowded lifeboat. Many of its people, mostly people of Indian extraction, suffer from malnutrition. Diarrhea caused by malnutrition is one of the leading causes of death there. Yet Guatemala has rich agricultural lands that are not being used to feed its people. Why is this so? Because the good land is being used to grow coffee and bananas for export to the developed countries of Europe and North America. Guatemalan coffee and bananas are not the only food products making their way from the underdeveloped to the developed world. There is in fact a net transfer of protein from the developing nations to the developed countries.[9] Then why don't the governments of Guatemala and other underdeveloped nations use their resources to feed their people? This has been tried. For example, in 1954 in Guatemala the democratically elected government of Jacob Arbenz attempted to redistribute some good land to poor farmers. The land redistribution was blocked by a military coup, a coup supported by the government of the United States. American support for the coup was arranged by the Central Intelligence Agency (CIA) during a time when the CIA was headed by Allen Dulles, brother of U.S. Secretary of State John Foster Dulles and member of the board of directors of United Fruit Company, an American company that owned land in Guatemala. Such features of the neocolonial order are surely morally relevant, but they are completely obscured by Hardin's lifeboat analogy.

## Public Goods and Collective Action

Despite the serious flaws in Hardin's argument, it turns on a theoretically interesting problem involving the relationship between individual action and what are called public goods, a problem that has ominous implications for the future of life on planet Earth. Consider the pasture shared by independent herders. Suppose I have one cow grazing on the pasture and I sell her milk at the end of each day. It occurs to me that I could double my income by adding more cows to my herd. Since the pasture costs me nothing, there is no additional cost. (Assume that herds can be increased for virtually nothing by refraining from slaughtering calves.) But presumably you and all the other herders who share the commons will be in the same position. So we all increase our herds. But now we have far too many cattle for the available forage. Though the incomes for each of us rise dramatically in the short run, eventually the pasture is overgrazed, we cannot feed our cattle, and we all lose. This is Hardin's "tragedy of the commons."

In this case, every individual's pursuit of self-interest combined to produce an outcome contrary to the self-interest of each. Suppose you see this. Should you then decide not to increase your herd? Not necessarily. Suppose enough of the other herders do decide to voluntarily restrict their herds. Then your increasing your herd will not cause overgrazing. So, in this case, you should add to your herd. Suppose, on the other hand, that most of the others do not curb the size of their herds. What should you do? If you don't increase the size of your herd, you will miss out on those short-term profits and suffer the disaster of overgrazing as well. As Durocher said, nice guys finish last. So you might as well add to your herd and at least reap your share of the short-term profits. Thus it appears that, even if you realize the possible disaster of everyone doing likewise, the individually rational thing for you to do is to increase the size of your herd. But clearly everyone else can reason in the same way. We seem, then, to have reached an impasse whereby each person acting rationally in his or her own self-interest is led to act in ways that produce a collective outcome contrary to the self-interest of each. What we have here is a problem of collective action.[10]

Problems of this kind are not at all uncommon. Suppose there is a beautiful plot of grass between your school and your favorite coffee shop. Should you walk across it? If enough people do, you will kill some of the grass and create an ugly muddy path. Still, you alone will make no difference. You alone walking across will not kill the grass. So if others don't, your doing so will cause no harm. But if others do, your not doing so will not cause any good. So you might as well. But then all others can reason likewise.

You work in a plant where labor is badly treated. There is talk of forming a union and going out on strike. If enough people join, the strike will be won and conditions will improve. Should you join? If you do and enough others don't, you will gain nothing and you risk being fired. If enough others do and you don't, you risk nothing and you share in the improved conditions. But if everyone thinks this way, you all lose the opportunity to improve working conditions.

Each of these cases can be seen as involving the provision of a collective good, a good such that if it is provided to one member of a group, it is necessarily provided to all members of the group as well. A union contract sets wages and working conditions for all who work in the plant. The green grassy area, if it is there at all, is there for the enjoyment of all who pass by. A lush common pasture, if it is there for any of us, is there for all of us. Such collective goods are different from private goods such as candy bars or shoes. If I consume the candy, no one else can do so. If I wear the shoes, no one else can do so without my giving them up. Collective goods are often called public goods because there are a number of such goods that have traditionally been provided by governmental agencies. Consider defense against foreign invasion and the provision of courts and police to maintain law and order. If such goods are provided at all, we all benefit from them. However, it should be noted that a thing can be a collective good without being something provided by government to the public as a whole, as for example the common pasture or the union contract. On the other hand, there are some goods typically provided by public agencies that are not really collective goods. Public schools provide educational instruction without a direct charge to the consumer, but it is possible to provide education as a private good paid for by the consumer and not the public.

## Public Goods, Markets, and Externalities

Since the time of Adam Smith, economists have recognized that public goods will not be provided by free markets. Suppose Dr. Strangelove invents a missile defense system that will shoot down enemy missiles with near-complete success. Unfortunately, the system is very expensive. Further, suppose the system will function as a public good. That is, if the system is set up, it will protect everyone within the borders of the country and not just those who pay for it. Suppose, for example, that it is prohibitively costly to arrange it so that it will shoot down only those missiles that threaten homes of those who have paid for the system. Now suppose Strangelove opens a Web site and offers the missile defense system for sale. Because of the expense, no individual or small group of individuals can afford it. Its purchase, then, will depend upon payment from a large number of individuals. Even though it is in the interest of each of us to have the system, each of us can reason that it is in our individual best interest not to pay for it, for if enough others pay we benefit anyway. Rational self-interest would lead each of us to act as a "free rider," enjoying the benefit of the public good but escaping our share of the cost. But since each of us can reason in this way, the system is likely to go unpurchased. The traditional solution to this sort of problem is for the government to buy the system and use its coercive power of taxation to force each of us who benefit to pay our fair share of the expense.

Because markets are unable to supply a public good, even though everyone in a society would prefer the good and would be willing to pay for it, the problem of public goods is often referred to as a market failure. Externalities also involve market failures. Negative externalities are costs incurred in the production of a good that do not appear in the market price of the good. Pollution is a classic example. Acid rain caused by coal-fired power plants may damage hardwood forests hundreds of miles away. A cost is incurred. Because the hardwood forest is damaged, the supply of hardwood is decreased, and the cost of hardwood is increased. But of course this cost is paid by consumers of hardwood, not by consumers of energy. In the free market, energy produced by coal-fired plants may be cheaper than energy produced by solar or wind power, though if the externalized costs were included in the reckoning, solar might be cheaper than coal. Because markets respond to market prices, not true costs including externalities, markets can inefficiently distribute scarce resources.

The classic solution to this kind of difficulty is to internalize the externalized cost, perhaps by requiring air scrubbers on smokestacks in coal-fired power plants and making the market cost correspond to the real cost of the energy produced. But, like public-goods problems, this too is likely to require the coercive intervention of government. Because internalization imposes costs on producers, and because competitive markets force producers to keep costs of production as low as possible, only coercive regulations requiring all producers to bear the costs are likely to succeed. In the last few decades this classic solution has been modified somewhat, with governmental agencies setting clean air standards and then granting saleable permits to pollute above these standards. This method allows for the use of market incentives to reduce pollution and reduces inefficiencies resulting from small gains purchased at heavy costs. However, this particular scheme still involves coercive governmental regulation.

## Planet Earth as a Public Good

We are now in a position to see the importance of the problems of collective action, public goods, and market externalities discussed above. A livable planet Earth is in the interest of every individual. Yet we live in a system of global capitalism based on free markets. We know that such a system is capable of producing negative externalities. We also know that such a system is not well designed for providing public goods.

Now consider the phenomena of global warming and depletion of the ozone layer. Both of these involve costs imposed on humankind and all other living things as well. They involve costs because they impose unwanted risks, conceivably including even the risk of the destruction of all human life. Global warming and depletion of the ozone layer are caused by substances released into the atmosphere as by-products of the production and consumption of goods sold on the open market. The costs they impose are not reflected in the market prices of those goods. They are thus market externalities. Internalization of these costs is likely to greatly increase the market prices of some commodities and is not likely to occur, as we have seen, without coercive regulation. At the same time, measures to clean the air and repair damage to the ozone, both public goods, are likely to be very expensive and likewise unprovided without coercive regulation.

All of this, however, leaves us with a very interesting difficulty. Briefly put, we live in a global capitalist system that relies on free markets to determine how resources will be utilized. Because of known market failures, free markets are likely to produce pollution and unlikely to produce public goods such as a livable planet Earth. The traditional solution to such problems involves coercive governmental interference with the market. But at present there is no governmental agency capable of imposing such controls on the global capitalist system. We appear to be heading for disaster.

## The Globalization Thesis

As the twentieth century draws to a close, one of the topics that has been much discussed concerns the phenomenon of globalization. The last few decades have seen a number of agreements to reduce or eliminate the remaining barriers to international trade and investment. Technological advancement in computers, computer networks, and communications have made it much easier to conduct business on a global scale. Responding to the ever-present competitive pressures of free markets and the ever-present rewards for cutting costs, corporations have taken advantage of the opportunities opened to them by the new international agreements and the new technologies. Increasingly, labor-intensive production processes have been transferred from developed countries, where the total costs of wages and benefits are high, to underdeveloped countries, where the total costs of wages and benefits are low. Such transfers also tend to reduce costs because of reduced environmental regulation in underdeveloped countries.

A number of critics have argued that this globalization of capitalism has undermined the ability of nation-states to control their economic fate. In a world of global competition, regulations and taxes imposed upon business by one nation to maintain high wages, limits to the working day, strong social safety nets, and high environmental standards raise costs of production within that nation, making indigenous firms less competitive on the world market. Challenged by overseas competitors with lower costs of production, firms have incentives to transfer their operations to other nations with less onerous regulations. The regulative strategies at the heart of new liberalism and the welfare state, strategies that turned on the use of governmental regulation and governmental power of redistributive taxation, appear to be ineffective in a world of global competition. In short, globalization appears to render the nation-state obsolete. In doing so, it also appears to have undercut the ability of a people to democratically control their fate. A nation whose people persist in voting for politicians who support traditional welfare-state commitments will find itself losing out in international competition and paying the price of increasing unemployment.[11]

Notice that the problem threatening here has structural similarities to the problems of collective action and collective goods discussed above. It may well be that no producer wants to lower the standard of living of workers, but each is forced to act in ways that produce that effect out of rational self-interest. The softhearted employer who insists on paying a living wage and controlling pollution will find himself driven out of business by his more ruthless competitors. Knowing that others are likely to act to reduce costs, the rational producer has no choice but to do likewise.

As we saw in our discussion of the problems of collective action, the traditional solution to such difficulties involves coercive regulation by governmental agencies. Minimum-wage laws, legal limits on the working day, health and safety regulations, and regulations requiring antipollution technologies all force each competitor to meet these standards. In effect, the regulations raise the costs of production for all producers, thereby preventing downward competition, whereby the ruthless competitor drags the good-hearted employer to his level.

The problem is that, just as there is no power able to impose global environmental regulations, so too there is no power able to impose regulations aimed at protecting wages, hours, and working conditions. In effect, global markets pit nation against nation in a struggle of downward competition. The nation that can promise companies the lowest taxes, lowest labor costs, and least costly environmental regulations wins the prospective industrial development. The nation that is more finicky in these matters loses out. Competing against one another to attract investment from global capitalism, nations are trapped in a downward competition, a race to the bottom, that threatens both workers' standards of living and environmental conditions.

## A Kantian Argument

Recognizing the potential for downward competition in free trade agreements, organized labor and environmental groups have sought to introduce regulation of working conditions and environmental regulations into international agreements to expand free trade. These proposals make eminent sense in light of the regulatory history of dealing with such problems within the confines of nation-state politics. So far such attempts have largely failed, with the small steps toward regulatory action actually taken producing only language that is vague and without effective enforcement mechanisms. Effective regulation has met with strong opposition from nation-states in the underdeveloped world, which see such regulation as interference with national sovereignty, and with opposition by powerful corporations, which view such regulation as unwarranted intrusion into the operation of the free market. There are some additional problems as well. Given the striking divide between the developed world and the underdeveloped world inherited from the age of imperialism, any imposition of uniform global standards regarding wages and benefits for workers and environmental regulations would almost surely work to stifle investment in the underdeveloped world. Globalization offers the promise of eventually overcoming the chasm that separates developed countries from underdeveloped ones. The trick is to see to it that globalization brings the underdeveloped world up rather than bringing the developed world down. Just how this trick can be done is quite another matter.

There is, however, yet another difficulty that must be faced. In the *Groundwork of the Metaphysic of Morals,* Immanuel Kant offered several distinct versions of what he took to be the underlying principle of all morality. One of those versions is formulated this way: "I ought never act except in such a way that I can also will that my maxim should become a universal law."[12] Though most philosophers reject Kant's own view that this principle provides a sufficient foundation for answering all moral questions, most philosophers do regard Kant's principle as a necessary condition for any morally acceptable action. That is, for it to be morally permissible for me to do X under circumstances Y, it must also be permissible for everyone else to do X under circumstances Y. My action must be "universalizable" if it is to be morally permissible. The force of this consideration is clear even to the child who is confronted with the question "What if everybody did that?"

But now consider this. In the countries of the developed world we have a way of life that is, despite some minor differences, more or less the same from one developed country to another. It is this way of life to which much of the underdeveloped world aspires, and it is this way of life we had in mind in saying that the trick is to lift the underdeveloped world up rather than pull the developed world down. In short, we aim at universalizing the way of life achieved in the advanced industrial world. But is this possible? Remember that the average citizen of the United States consumes thirty times as much of the earth's resources as the average person of Bangladesh. There are good reasons for thinking that this high-consumption way of life cannot be universalized without bringing ecological disaster to planet Earth.[13] The conclusion implied by these premises, and the Kantian principle of universalizability, is that the way of life we all enjoy in the developed world is not morally acceptable and that therefore we ought to make major changes in it.

On the other hand, there is another widely accepted principle of ethics that says that "ought implies can." We cannot be obligated to do something that is impossible for us to do. Many philosophers have interpreted "impossible" in terms of what is unreasonably demanding. On this "morality lite" understanding of the principle, we cannot be obligated to make the changes in our way of life apparently demanded by the Kantian principle since those changes make unreasonable demands upon us.

Those of us in the developed world may take some comfort in this reply. It seems to save us from the hard demands of the Kantian principle. But people in the underdeveloped world may not be so easily reconciled to present arrangements. Seeing that current arrangements fail the Kantian test of universalizability, they may appeal to the traditional principles of social-contract theory, according to which large and persistent injustices absolve aggrieved parties from the duties imposed by the contract.

# ── Chapter 11 ──

# Some Concluding Thoughts

It is only now, in the waning days of the twentieth century, that something like a universal history of the world begins. Heretofore Asia, Africa, Europe, and the New World had, to a large extent, their separate histories. Now those histories have come together. The events of the last five hundred years have knit the fates of all humankind together. From this point forward we share a single history.

History is not like the movements of the planets around the stars or the changing of the seasons. There repetition reigns eternal. History never repeats itself. This is not to say that history somehow escapes the chains of causation, though it might for all I know. But even if causation rules history, still history never repeats itself. It is a unique and singular process. The boulder cascading down the mountainside is surely bound by the laws of nature. There are causes for why it falls when, where, and how it does. But there are no laws of boulder-falling-down-mountain motion the way there are laws of planetary motion. To be sure, if we were to duplicate exactly the conditions under which a boulder fell, we would get exactly the same result. But the conditions never are the same. And in history they cannot be the same, either. Hegel rightly ridicules the saying that those who do not know the past are condemned to repeat it.[1] The present is never like the past, if only because its history is different. Determined not to make the mistakes of the past, we fail to notice this—that the present is not the past. The architects of American involvement in Vietnam were determined to avoid the errors of Munich. The generation that suffered the tragedy of Vietnam is determined not to repeat that mistake.

To say that now humankind begins a truly universal history is not to say that somehow all human differences have been canceled out and that we are henceforth all of one gender, race, nation, and religion. It is to say that people of different genders, races, nations, and religions must now work out a future they all share. The task of political philosophy is to say what the rules of life governing that future should be and what the institutions making and enforcing those rules should be like. Political philosophy can no longer be thought of in terms of the institutions of an ideal state. The universal history of the future transcends the nation-state.

Like it or not, the threads that have united us are the markets of global capitalism. The world capitalist system, forged in the era of imperialism and scarred by the ugly divide between the developed and the underdeveloped world, is the foundation upon which this universal history must be built. The task of political philosophy is to think through where we go from here. To do that will require a deep understanding of the defective foundation upon which we build, a respect for the perspectives of people other than ourselves, an understanding of the ecological limits to human action, and a serious study of economics.

Political philosophy understood in this way is a form of reflective, situated thought. It is situated in the historical context, and it attempts a wide-ranging reflection on this context.

But though political philosophy is historically situated, it is not historically relative. Political philosophy aims at understanding the truth about the present and at recommending a path for the future. For this the objective canons of empirical truth, logical validity, and the universally acknowledged principles of elementary morality suffice, though the work of thinking it all through demands great effort.

The attentive reader will have noticed that the study offered here shines no light at all onto the future. Nowhere in these pages have we found a way forward. Instead, we seem to have discovered obstacles everywhere. Neither the facile optimism of free markets nor blind faith in the welfare state seems to provide a safe path into the future; nor do conservative theocracies, whether Moslem or Christian. It is ironic that we moderns, living in the peace and comfort of the present, are less optimistic than Condorcet, in hiding from the guillotine. The task of political philosophy is not an easy one. The reader will have to carry on alone from here.

# Notes

## Chapter 1

1. Howard H. Peckham, *The War for Independence: A Military History,* p. 8.
2. Arthur B. Tourtellot's *Lexington and Concord* provides a rich account of the confrontation at Lexington and the local background leading up to it.
3. Ibid., p. 43.
4. Ibid., p. 44.
5. For Jefferson's reply to this charge, see his letter to James Madison of August 30, 1823, in *The Writings of Thomas Jefferson,* Volume XV, p. 462.
6. The philosophical analysis that follows is heavily indebted to Morton White, *The Philosophy of the American Revolution.* Readers who would like to pursue questions in more detail are urged to consult White's admirable work.
7. John Locke, *Second Treatise,* Chapter II, Section 4.
8. Quoted in White, p. 73.
9. John Locke, *An Essay Concerning Human Understanding,* Book IV, Chapter II, Section 1.
10. John Locke, *Second Treatise,* Chapter II, Section 5.

## Chapter 2

1. Adam Smith, *An Inquiry into the Nature and Causes of the Wealth of Nations,* p. 3.
2. Ibid., p. 423.
3. Elie Halévy, *The Growth of Philosophical Radicalism,* pp. 174–175.
4. Jeremy Bentham, *Anarchical Fallacies,* p. 501.
5. Jeremy Bentham, *An Introduction to the Principles of Morals and Legislation,* p. 19.
6. Ibid., Chapter XIV, Note 1, Section 7.
7. This phrase comes from Chapter 4 of Bentham's *Principles,* where Bentham considers the ideal utilitarian calculus and the variables relevant to it.

## Chapter 3

1. John Locke, *The Second Treatise of Government*, Chapter VIII.
2. Elie Halévy, *The Growth of Philosophical Radicalism*, p. 144.
3. Ibid., p. 141.
4. On Hume's argument, see Halévy, pp. 120, 132–133.
5. Halévy, p. 141.
6. Ibid., p. 172.
7. Ibid., p. 419.
8. John Stuart Mill, *On Liberty*, pp. 196–197.
9. Ibid., p. 198.
10. J. Salwyn Schapiro, *Condorcet and the Rise of Liberalism*, p. 76.
11. Ibid., pp. 76, 158–167.
12. Ibid., p. 84.
13. Ibid., pp. 106–107.
14. Antoine-Nicolas de Condorcet, *Sketch for a Historical Picture of the Progress of the Human Mind*, p. 201.
15. Schapiro, p. 262.

## Chapter 4

1. Another classic description of the lives of working-class people in the time of early capitalism can be found in Frederick Engels, *Condition of the Working Class in England*, published originally in 1844.
2. John Locke, *Second Treatise*, Chapter V, Section 27.
3. For a very interesting discussion of this and other problems related to Locke's labor theory of original acquisition, see Robert Nozick, *Anarchy, State, and Utopia*, pp. 174–182.
4. P.J. Proudhon, *General Idea of the Revolution in the Nineteenth Century* (1851), quoted in Nozick, p. 11 n.
5. John Locke, *Second Treatise*, Chapter 5, Section 28.
6. Adam Smith, *An Inquiry into the Nature and Causes of the Wealth of Nations*, p. 47; David Ricardo, *The Principles of Political Economy*, pp. 6–7.
7. Among those who advanced this argument were Thomas Hodgskin, William Thompson, Francis Bray, and John Gray. On these Ricardian socialists, see Maurice Dobb, *Theories of Value and Distribution Since Adam Smith*, pp. 137–141.
8. Acts 4:32–35. For the story of the young rich man, see Mark 10:17–25.
9. Karl Marx and Frederick Engels, *Manifesto of the Communist Party*, p. 48.
10. The classic expression of this broader conception of the direction of history is found in the preface to Karl Marx's *Contribution to the Critique of Political Economy*, published in 1859.
11. In the *Manifesto* Marx lists a sample ten-point program for the transition period. The idea of a transition period appears also in Marx's *Critique of the Gotha Program*, written in 1875, as does the quoted slogan regarding distribution. The idea of socialism as providing the conditions for the free development of all is from the last sentence of Part II of the *Manifesto*.

12. Marx and Engels, *Manifesto*, p. 59.
13. Karl Marx, "Amsterdam Speech," p. 523.
14. V.I. Lenin, *What Is to Be Done?* (1902).

## Chapter 5

1. Herbert Spencer, "From Freedom to Bondage," in Julia Stapleton, ed., *Liberalism, Democracy, and the State in Britain*, pp. 135–157.
2. Derek Fraser, *The Evolution of the British Welfare State*, p. 109.
3. Adolph Wagner, "Speech on the Social Question to the Assembly of Evangelical Free Churchmen" (October 1871), in Donald Wagner, ed., *Social Reformers*, p. 503.
4. Quoted in James Rachels, *Elements of Moral Philosophy*, p. 133.
5. On neo-Kantian socialism, see Harry Van Der Linden, *Kantian Ethics and Socialism*.
6. T.H. Green, "Liberal Legislation and Freedom of Contract," in Julia Stapleton, ed., *Liberalism, Democracy, and the State in Britain*, pp. 112–113.
7. H.J. Laski, *The Decline of Liberalism* (1940), quoted by W.H. Greenleaf, *The British Political Tradition*, Vol. 2, p. 124.
8. John Stuart Mill, *On Liberty*, p. 197.
9. T.H. Green, "Liberal Legislation and Freedom of Contract," p. 117.
10. In W.H. Greenleaf, *The British Political Tradition*, Vol. 2, p. 136.
11. L.T. Hobhouse, *Liberalism* (1911).
12. Robert B. Westbrook, *John Dewey and American Democracy*, p. 43.
13. A.D. Lindsay, "Introduction," to T.H. Green, *Principles of Political Obligation*, p. v.
14. Karl Marx and Frederick Engels, *Manifesto of the Communist Party*, 76.
15. John Stuart Mill, *Utilitarianism*, pp. 331–332.
16. Green, "Liberal Legislation and Freedom of Contract," p. 113.
17. Adam Smith, *Wealth of Nations*, p. 66.
18. L.T. Hobhouse, *Liberalism*, p. 50.

## Chapter 6

1. L.T. Hobhouse, *Liberalism*, p. 105.
2. For a discussion of the history of theories of taxation and of the progressive income tax in particular, see Harold Groves, *Tax Philosophers*.
3. Immanuel Kant, *Groundwork of the Metaphysic of Morals*, p. 96.
4. For an excellent discussion of these issues, see James Rachels, *Elements of Moral Philosophy*, pp. 110–115.
5. Karl Marx, *Critique of the Gotha Program*, in Lewis S. Feuer, ed., *Marx and Engels: Basic Writings On Politics And Philosophy*, p. 117.
6. Ibid., p. 119.
7. Ibid.
8. On the use of piece-rate incentives in the Soviet Union, see Alec Nove, *The Soviet Economy*, pp. 122.

9. John Rawls, *A Theory of Justice*, p. 302.

10. For Rawls's reasoning concerning the priority of liberty, see *A Theory of Justice*, pp. 541–548.

11. Ibid., pp. 302–303. See also p. 89.

12. James P. Sterba, *The Demands of Justice.*

13. Ronald Dworkin, "What Is Equality? Part I: Equality of Welfare," and "What Is Equality? Part II: Equality of Resources."

## Chapter 7

1. Robert Nozick, *Anarchy, State, and Utopia.*

2. This is a somewhat updated version of Nozick's own famous example based on the great basketball player Wilt Chamberlain. See Nozick, pp. 160–164.

3. Ibid., p. 163.

4. John Stuart Mill, *On Liberty*, p. 197.

5. T.H. Green, "Liberal Legislation and Freedom of Contract," p. 117.

6. National Resources Planning Board Report (December 16, 1942), in Henry Steele Commager, ed., *Documents of American History*, p. 673.

7. The UN Declaration and a number of other related documents can be found in Walter Laqueur and Barry Rubin, eds., *The Human Rights Reader.*

8. Quoted in W.H. Greenleaf, *The British Political Tradition* Vol. 2, p. 138. On Dicey, see also Julia Stapleton, ed., *Liberalism, Democracy and the State*, p. 19.

9. Herbert Spencer, "From Freedom to Bondage," pp. 135–157.

10. Friedrich A. Hayek, *The Road to Serfdom;* Milton Friedman, *Capitalism and Freedom.*

11. Perhaps her most philosophical work is Ayn Rand, *The Virtue of Selfishness.*

12. John Stuart Mill, *On Liberty*, p. 198.

13. Nozick, *Anarchy, State, and Utopia*, p. ix.

14. John Hospers, "What Libertarianism Is" (1974), p. 3.

15. John Hospers, "What Libertarianism Is" (1995), p. 8.

16. Jan Narveson, *The Libertarian Idea*, p. 7.

17. For an excellent introductory discussion of the critique of utilitarianism and attempts to defend utilitarianism against these criticisms, see James Rachels, *The Elements of Moral Philosophy*, pp. 107–121.

18. For further discussion of the distinction between teleological and deontological theories, see William Frankena, *Ethics*, pp. 13–16. Rawls himself notes that his theory is deontological because it lacks the teleological structure of utilitarianism, but he is critical of many of the standard ways of characterizing this distinction and its importance. See John Rawls, *A Theory of Justice*, pp. 30, 40.

19. Michael Freeden, *Rights.*

20. Ayn Rand, *The Virtue of Selfishness*, quoted in Hospers, "What Libertarianism Is" (1995), p. 11.

21. The radical implications of libertarian theory for positive rights and for the role of unions is clearly formulated in John Hospers, "What Libertarianism Is" (1974).

# Chapter 8

1. The reference to the gulag and the Holocaust comes from the libertarian philosopher Loren Lomasky, in Tibor R. Machan and Douglas B. Rasmussen, eds., *Liberty for the Twenty-First Century*, p. ix.

2. On Burke's criticism of the doctrines of natural law and natural rights that inspired the American and French Revolutions, see Peter J. Stanlis, *Edmund Burke and the Natural Law*. Burke, of course, supported the American revolution, though not the doctrine of natural rights found in the Declaration of Independence.

3. That "ought" cannot be derived from "is" is one of the famous insights of the philosopher David Hume. See his *Treatise of Human Nature* (1739–40), Book III, Part I, Section I, paragraph 504.

4. For a discussion of Locke's argument, see Morton White, *The Philosophy of the American Revolution*, pp. 70–75.

5. This may be so, but Bentham's utilitarianism is itself bedeviled by the is/ought problem. From the fact that only happiness is intrinsically valuable it does not at all follow that we ought to promote happiness.

6. John Hospers, "What Libertarianism Is" (1974), p. 3.

7. The most prominent defender of this approach is David Gauthier, *Morals by Agreement*. See also Jan Narveson, *The Libertarian Idea*.

8. Nozick, *Anarchy, State, and Utopia*, pp. 30–31.

9. On American Indian beliefs, see W.C. Vanderwerth, *Indian Oratory*, pp. 4–5. On Jefferson, see "Jefferson to James Madison, September 6, 1789," in *The Portable Thomas Jefferson*, p. 445.

10. John Hospers, "What Libertarianism Is" (1995), p. 10.

11. Robert Nozick, *Anarchy, State, and Utopia*, pp. 174–175.

12. Ayn Rand, *The Virtue of Selfishness*, p. 94.

13. Jan Narveson, "Contracting for Liberty," p. 27.

14. John Locke, *Second Treatise*, Chapter 5, Section 27.

15. Nozick, *Anarchy, State, and Utopia*, p. 176.

16. Ibid., p. 177.

17. Ibid., pp. 178–179 (note on Fourier).

18. Jan Narveson, "Contracting for Liberty," p. 27.

19. This example is freely borrowed from Cheyney Ryan, "Yours, Mine, and Ours: Property Rights and Individual Liberty."

20. For a discussion of this distinction in the history of natural-law theory and its influence on Thomas Jefferson, see Morton White, *The Philosophy of the American Revolution*, pp. 213–228.

21. Ludwig von Mises, *Human Action: A Treatise on Economics;* Friedrich A. Hayek, *The Road to Serfdom;* Milton Friedman, *Capitalism and Freedom.*

22. John Hospers, "What Libertarianism Is" (1974), p. 20.

23. Friedrich A. Hayek, *Capitalism and the Historians.*

24. Friedrich A. Hayek, *Prices and Production.*

25. Milton Friedman and Rose Friedman, *Free to Choose*, pp. 70–90.

26. Peter Singer, "Famine, Affluence, and Morality," p. 407.

27. L.T. Hobhouse, *Liberalism*, p. 105.

28. Immanuel Kant, "Theory and Practice," in *The Philosophy of Kant*, pp. 412–429.

29. Immanuel Kant, *Kant's Political Writings*, p. 149.

## Chapter 9

1. An excellent account of the historical origins of patriarchal social systems can be found in Gerda Lerner, *The Creation of Patriarchy*.

2. Plato questions the supposed superiority of men over women in Book Five of *The Republic*.

3. Aristotle, *Politics*, Book I.

4. American Council of Learned Societies, *Dictionary of Scientific Biography*, Vol. 6, pp. 615–616. *Hypatia* is the name of one of the leading journals of feminist philosophy at this time.

5. Aristotle, *Politics*, Book I, Chapter 5.

6. Mary Wollstonecraft, *A Vindication of the Rights of Women*.

7. Jean-Jacques Rousseau, *Emile*, quoted in Mary Mahowald, ed., *Philosophy of Woman*, p. 89.

8. On Kant's racism, see Tsenay Serequeberhan, "The Critique of Eurocentrism," pp. 148–149. On Linnaeus, see Léon Poliakov, *The Aryan Myth*, p. 161.

9. Frederick Douglass, "What to the Slave Is the Fourth of July," in *The Frederick Douglass Papers*, p. 370.

10. For Freud's views and critical assessment of them by Karen Horney see Mary Mahowald, ed., *Philosophy of Woman*, pp. 224–241, 245–256.

11. For critical histories of this "scientific" racism, see Léon Poliakov, *The Aryan Myth*, and Stephen Jay Gould, *The Mismeasure of Man*.

12. Charles Murray, "Affirmative Racism," and Richard J. Herrnstein and Charles Murray, *The Bell Curve*. There are a number of books critical of the claims advanced by Herrnstein and Murray. Among them are Steven Fraser, ed., *The Bell Curve Wars*, and Claude Fisher et al., *Inequality by Design: Cracking the Bell Curve Myth*.

13. Abigail Adams to John Adams, March 31, 1776, in H. Butterfield, et al., eds., *The Book of Abigail and John*, pp. 120–122.

14. Susan Okin, *Justice, Gender, and the Family*, p. 161.

15. Frantz Fanon, *The Wretched of the Earth*.

16. For an introduction to contemporary feminist philosophy, see Eve Browning Cole, *Philosophy and Feminist Criticism*. Leonard Harris's *Philosophy Born of Struggle* provides a point of entry into contemporary African-American philosophy.

17. The foundations of Habermas's thought are presented in Jürgen Habermas, *The Theory of Communicative Action*. A more accessible introduction is Jürgen Habermas, *Legitimation Crisis*.

18. John 8:32.

19. For an anthology of papers dealing with related themes, see Louise M. Antony and Charlotte Witt, eds., *A Mind of One's Own: Feminist Essays on Reason and Objectivity*. Iris Young, in *Justice and the Politics of Difference*, develops a position that draws from the tradition of critical theory and incorporates postmodernist ideas.

## Chapter 10

1. W.E.B. DuBois, *Souls of Black Folk*, p. 23.

2. The Vietnamese Declaration of Independence, proclaimed in 1946 and written by Ho Chi Minh, quotes directly from the American Declaration and refers to the American Declaration as asserting that all the peoples of the earth are equal from birth. "Declaration of Independence of the Democratic Republic of Vietnam," in George Kahn and John Lewis, eds., *The United States in Vietnam*, p. 419.

3. See David Forsythe, *Human Rights and World Politics*, p. 177.

4. For critical surveys of all of these theories of imperialism, see Anthony Brewer, *Marxist Theories of Imperialism* and Charles Barone, *Marxist Thought on Imperialism*.

5. Garrett Hardin, "Living on a Lifeboat," p. 414.

6. Ibid., p. 416.

7. Arthur Simon, *Bread for the World*, p. 41, cited by Robert Van Wyk in "Perspective on World Hunger and the Extent of Our Positive Duties," p. 424.

8. Van Wyk, p. 422.

9. Ibid.

10. Mancur Olson's *The Logic of Collective Action* is the classic study of these problems.

11. Among important contributions to the analysis of globalization are Robert B. Reich, *The Work of Nations;* Susan Strange, *The Retreat of the State;* and Paul Hirst and Graham Thompson, *Globalization in Question*. For a criticism of the globalization argument, see Linda Weiss, "The Myth of the Powerless State."

12. Immanuel Kant, *Groundwork of the Metaphysics of Morals*, p. 70.

13. See Adam Swift, *Global Political Ecology*.

## Chapter 11

1. G.W.F. Hegel, *Introduction to the Philosophy of History*, p. 8.

# Bibliography

American Council of Learned Societies. *Dictionary of Scientific Biography,* Vol. 6. New York: Charles Scribner's Sons, 1972.

Antony, Louise M., and Charlotte Witt, eds. *A Mind of One's Own: Feminist Essays on Reason and Objectivity.* Boulder, CO: Westview, 1993.

Aristotle. *Politics.* In *The Works of Aristotle.* New York: Random House, 1970.

Barone, Charles. *Marxist Thought on Imperialism.* Armonk, NY: M.E. Sharpe, 1985.

Bentham, Jeremy. *Anarchical Fallacies.* In *The Works of Jeremy Bentham,* Vol. 2, ed. John Bowring. New York: Russell and Russell, 1962.

———. *An Introduction to the Principles of Morals and Legislation.* New York: Haffner, 1948.

Brewer, Anthony. *Marxist Theories of Imperialism.* London: Routledge, 1989.

Butterfield, H., et al., eds. *The Book of Abigail and John.* Cambridge: Harvard University Press, 1977.

Cole, Eve Browning. *Philosophy and Feminist Criticism.* New York: Paragon, 1993.

Commager, Henry Steele, ed. *Documents of American History.* New York: Appleton-Century-Crofts, 1948.

Condorcet, Antoine-Nicolas de. *Sketch for a Historical Picture of the Progress of the Human Mind.* London: Weidenfeld and Nicolson, 1955.

Dobb, Maurice. *Theories of Value and Distribution Since Adam Smith.* Cambridge: Cambridge University Press, 1973.

Douglass, Frederick. *The Frederick Douglass Papers,* Vol. 2., ed. John W. Blassingame. New Haven: Yale University Press, 1982.

DuBois, W.E.B. *Souls of Black Folk.* New York: Fawcett, 1968.

Dworkin, Ronald. "What Is Equality? Part I: Equality of Welfare." *Philosophy and Public Affairs* 10, no. 3 (1981): 185–246.

———. "What Is Equality? Part II: Equality of Resources." *Philosophy and Public Affairs* 10, no. 4 (1981): 283–345.

Engels, Frederick. *Condition of the Working Class in England.* London: George Allen and Unwin, 1950.

Fanon, Frantz. *The Wretched of the Earth.* New York: Grove, 1963.

Feuer, Lewis S., ed. *Marx and Engels: Basic Writings on Politics and Philosophy.* Garden City: Anchor, 1959.

Fisher, Claude, et al. *Inequality by Design: Cracking the Bell Curve Myth.* Princeton: Princeton University Press, 1996.

Forsythe, David. *Human Rights and World Politics.* Lincoln: University of Nebraska Press, 1989.

Frankena, William. *Ethics.* Englewood Clifts, NJ: Prentice Hall, 1963.

Fraser, Derek. *The Evolution of the British Welfare State.* New York: Macmillan, 1973.

Fraser, Steven, ed. *The Bell Curve Wars.* New York: Basic Books, 1995.

Freeden, Michael. *Rights.* Minneapolis: University of Minnesota Press, 1991.

Friedman, Milton. *Capitalism and Freedom.* Chicago: University of Chicago Press, 1962.

Friedman, Milton, and Rose Friedman. *Free to Choose.* New York: Harcourt Brace Jovanovich, 1980.

Gauthier, David. *Morals by Agreement.* Oxford: Oxford University Press, 1986.

Gould, Stephen Jay. *The Mismeasure of Man.* New York: Norton, 1981.

Green, Thomas Hill. "Liberal Legislation and Freedom of Contract." In J. Stapleton, ed., *Liberalism, Democracy, and the State in Britain: Five Essays, 1862–1891.* Bristol: Thoemmes, 1997.

———. *Principles of Political Obligation.* Ann Arbor: University of Michigan Press, 1967.

Greenleaf, W.H. *The British Political Tradition,* Vol. 2. London: Methuen, 1983.

Groves, Harold M. *Tax Philosophers.* Madison, WI: University of Wisconsin Press, 1974.

Habermas, Jürgen. *The Theory of Communicative Action.* Boston: Beacon Press, 1983.

———. *Legitimation Crisis.* Boston: Beacon Press, 1973.

Halévy, Elie. *The Growth of Philosophical Radicalism.* Clifton, NJ: Augustus M. Kelley, 1972.

Hardin, George. "Living on a Lifeboat." In Thomas Mappes and Jane Zembaty, eds., *Social Ethics.* New York: McGraw-Hill, 1992.

Harris, Leonard. *Philosophy Born of Struggle.* Dubuque: Kendall/Hunt, 1993.

Hayek, Friedrich A. *The Road to Serdom.* Chicago: University of Chicago Press, 1944.

———. *Prices and Production.* London: Routledge, 1931.

———. *Capitalism and the Historians.* Chicago: University of Chicago Press, 1954.

Hegel, G.W.F. *Introduction to the Philosophy of History.* Indianapolis: Hackett, 1988.

Herrnstein, Richard, and Charles Murray. *The Bell Curve.* New York: Free Press, 1994.

Hirst, Paul, and Graham Thompson. *Globalization in Question.* Cambridge: Blackwell, 1996.

Hobhouse, L.T. *Liberalism.* Oxford: Oxford University Press, 1964.

Hospers, John. "What Libertarianism Is" (1995). In Tibor Machan and Douglas Rasmussen, eds., *Liberty for the Twenty-First Century.* Boston: Rowan and Littlefield, 1995.

————. "What Libertarianism Is" (1974) In Tibor Machan, ed., *The Libertarian Alternative*. Chicago: Nelson-Hall, 1974.

Hume, David. *Treatise of Human Nature*. Oxford: Clarendon Press, 1967.

Jefferson, Thomas. *The Portable Thomas Jefferson,* ed. Merrill D. Peterson. New York: Penguin, 1980.

————. *The Writings of Thomas Jefferson,* eds. A.A. Lipscomb and A.E. Bergh. Washington: 1903.

Kahn, George, and John Lewis. *The United States in Vietnam*. New York: Delta Books, 1969.

Kant, Immanuel. *The Philosophy of Kant: Immanuel Kant's Moral and Political Writings*. New York: Modern Library, 1977.

————. *Kant's Political Writings*. Cambridge: Cambridge University Press, 1971.

————. *Groundwork of the Metaphysic of Morals*. New York: Harper and Row, 1964.

Laqueur, Walter, and Barry Rubin, eds. *The Human Rights Reader* New York: Meridian, 1990.

Lenin, V.I. *What Is to Be Done?* Moscow: Progress, 1973.

Lerner, Gerda. *The Creation of Patriarchy*. New York: Oxford University Press, 1986.

Locke, John. *An Essay Concerning Human Understanding*. London: J.M. Dent and Sons, 1967.

————. *Second Treaties,* in *Two Treatises of Government*. New York: New American Library, 1965.

Machan, Tibor R., and Douglas B. Rasmussen, eds. *Liberty for the Twenty-First Century*. Boston: Rowan and Littlefield, 1995.

Mahowald, Mary, ed. *Philosophy of Woman*. Indianapolis: Hackett, 1994.

Mappes, Thomas, and Jane Zembaty, eds. *Social Ethics*. New York: McGraw-Hill, 1992.

Marx, Karl A. *A Contribution to the Critique of Political Economy*. New York: International, 1972.

————. "Amsterdam Speech." In *The Marx-Engels Reader,* ed. Robert Tucker. New York: Norton, 1978.

————. *Critique of the Gotha Program*. In Marx, Karl, and Engels, Frederick, *Marx and Engels: Basic Writings on Politics and Philosophy,* ed. Lewis Feuer. Garden City, NY: Doubleday, 1959.

Marx, Karl, and Frederick Engels. *Marx and Engels: Basic Writings on Politics and Philosophy,* ed. Lewis Feuer. Garden City, NY: Doubleday, 1959.

————. *Manifesto of the Communist Party*. Moscow: Progress, 1977.

Mill, John Stuart. *Utilitarianism*. In *The Philosophy of John Stuart Mill*. New York: Modern Library, 1961.

————. *On Liberty*. In *The Philosophy of John Stuart Mill*. New York: Modern Library, 1961.

Murray, Charles. "Affirmative Racism." *The New Republic,* December 31, 1984, pp. 18–23.

Narveson, Jan. "Contracting for Liberty." In Tibor Machan and Douglas Rasmussen, eds., *Liberty for the Twenty-First Century*. Boston: Rowan and Littlefield, 1995.

————. *The Libertarian Idea*. Philadelphia: Temple University Press, 1988.

Nove, Alec. *The Soviet Economy*. New York: Praeger, 1966.

Nozick, Robert. *Anarchy, State, and Utopia*. New York: Basic Books, 1974.

Okin, Susan. *Justice, Gender and the Family*. New York: Basic Books, 1989.

Olson, Mancur. *The Logic of Collective Action*. New York: Schocken, 1970.

Peckham, Howard H. *The War for Independence: A Military History*. Chicago: University of Chicago Press, 1958.

Plato. *The Republic*. New York: Modern Library. n.d.

Poliakov, Léon. *The Aryan Myth*. New York: Basic Books, 1971.

Rachels, James. *Elements of Moral Philosophy*. Boston: McGraw-Hill, 1999.

Rand, Ayn. *The Virtue of Selfishness*. New York: Harper and Row, 1968.

Rawls, John. *A Theory of Justice*. Cambridge: Harvard University Press, 1971.

Reich, Robert B. *The Work of Nations*. New York: Random House, 1992.

Ricardo, David. *The Principles of Political Economy*. London: Everyman, 1962.

Ryan, Cheyney. "Yours, Mine, and Ours: Property Rights and Individual Liberty." *Ethics* 87 (January 1977): 126–141.

Schapiro, J. Salwyn. *Condorcet and the Rise of Liberalism*. New York: Harcourt, Brace, 1934.

Serequeberhan, Tsenay. "The Critique of Eurocentrism." In Emmanuel Chukwudi Eze, ed., *Postcolonial African Philosophy*. Oxford: Blackwell, 1997.

Singer, Peter. "Famine, Affluence, and Morality." In Thomas Mappes and Jane Zembaty, eds., *Social Ethics*. New York: McGraw-Hill, 1992.

Smith, Adam. *An Inquiry into the Nature and Causes of the Wealth of Nations*. New York: Modern Library, 1937.

Spencer, Herbert. "From Freedom to Bondage." In J. Stapleton, ed., *Liberalism, Democracy, and the State in Britain: Five Essays, 1862–1891*. Bristol: Thoemmes.

Stanlis, Peter J. *Edmund Burke and the Natural Law*. Lafayette, LA: Huntington House, 1986.

Stapleton, Julia, ed. *Liberalism, Democracy, and the State in Britain: Five Essays, 1862–1891*. Bristol: Thoemmes, 1997.

Sterba, James. *The Demands of Justice*. Notre Dame: University of Notre Dame Press, 1980.

Strange, Susan. *The Retreat of the State*. Cambridge: Cambridge University Press, 1996.

Swift, Adam. *Global Political Ecology*. London: Pluto, 1993.

Tourtellot, Arthur B. *Lexington and Concord*. New York: Norton, 1963.

Van Der Linden, Harry. *Kantian Ethics and Socialism*. Indianapolis: Hackett, 1988.

Vanderwerth, W.C. *Indian Oratory*. Norman: University of Oklahoma Press, 1971.

Van Wyk, Robert. "Prospectives on World Hunger and the Extent of Our Positive Duties." In Thomas Mappes and Jane Zembaty, eds., *Social Ethics*. New York: McGraw-Hill, 1992.

von Mises, Ludwig. *Human Action: A Treatise on Economics*. New Haven: Yale University Press, 1949.

Wagner, Adolph. "Speech on the Social Question to the Assembly of Evangelical Free Churchmen." In Donald Wagner, ed., *Social Reformers*. New York: Macmillan, 1947.

Weiss, Linda. "The Myth of the Powerless State." *New Left Review* 225 (September/October 1997): 3–27.

Westbrook, Robert B. *John Dewey and American Democracy.* Ithaca, NY: Cornell University Press, 1991.

White, Morton. *The Philosophy of the American Revolution.* New York: Oxford University Press, 1978.

Wollstonecraft, Mary. *A Vindication of the Rights of Women.* Buffalo: Prometheus, 1989.

Young, Iris Marion. *Justice and the Politics of Difference.* Princeton: Princeton University Press, 1990.

# Index

# About the Author

**Richard Hudelson** received his Ph.D. in philosophy in 1977 from the University of Michigan. He is currently Senior Lecturer in Philosophy at the University of Wisconsin Superior. He is the author of *Marxism and Philosophy in the Twentieth Century* (1990) and *The Rise and Fall of Communism* (1993) as well as numerous articles and reviews in the fields of political philosophy and philosophy of the social sciences.